D1207491

At Issue

What Is the Future of the U.S. Economy?

Other Books in the At Issue Series:

At Issue

What Is the Future of the U.S. Economy?

Susan C. Hunnicutt, Book Editor

GREENHAVEN PRESS
A part of Gale, Cengage Learning

GALE
CENGAGE Learning

Detroit • New York • San Francisco • New Haven, Conn • Waterville, Maine • London

GALE
CENGAGE Learning™

Christine Nasso, *Publisher*
Elizabeth Des Chenes, *Managing Editor*

© 2008 Greenhaven Press, a part of Gale, Cengage Learning.

Gale and Greenhaven Press are registered trademarks used herein under license.

For more information, contact:
Greenhaven Press
27500 Drake Rd.
Farmington Hills, MI 48331-3535
Or you can visit our Internet site at gale.cengage.com

For product information and technology assistance, contact us at

Gale Customer Support, 1-800-877-4253
For permission to use material from this text or product, submit all requests online at
www.cengage.com/permissions

Further permissions questions can be emailed to permissionrequest@cengage.com

Articles in Greenhaven Press anthologies are often edited for length to meet page requirements. In addition, original titles of these works are changed to clearly present the main thesis and to explicitly indicate the author's opinion. Every effort is made to ensure that Greenhaven Press accurately reflects the original intent of the authors. Every effort has been made to trace the owners of copyrighted material.

Cover photograph reproduced by permission of Images.com/Corbis.

LIBRARY OF CONGRESS CATALOGING-IN-PUBLICATION DATA

What is the future of the U.S. economy? / Susan C. Hunnicutt, book editor.
  p. cm. -- (At issue)
  Includes bibliographical references and index.
  ISBN-13: 978-0-7377-3942-8 (hardcover)
  ISBN-13: 978-0-7377-3943-5 (pbk.)
  1. United States--Economic conditions--2001- 2. United States--Economic policy
--2001- I. Hunnicutt, Susan.
  HC106.83.W46 2008
  330.973--dc22
                                                    2008001002

330.973 HUN 2008

What is the future of the
U.S. economy?

Printed in the United States of America
1 2 3 4 5 6 7 12 11 10 09 08

Contents

Introduction

The American Dream is a symbol with deep roots in the American psyche. The idea that prosperity is within the reach of everyone through a combination of thrift, diligence, and hard work is one that can be traced to many iconic figures in the history of the United States: Ben Franklin's *Poor Richard* dispensed commonsense economic advice to ordinary people in the mid-eighteenth century. Franklin made a name for himself purveying pithy aphorisms such as "Early to bed and early to rise makes a man healthy, wealthy, and wise," and "Industry pays debts." Later, Abraham Lincoln declared his belief that the North's industrial economy was the ultimate source of its greatness, since it created the opportunity for all to prosper. After the American Civil War, popular storyteller Horatio Alger offered up spirited characters who parlayed perseverance and hard work into secure futures for themselves and their families, and in the 1950s and 1960s, African American preacher Martin Luther King insisted that the promise of the American Dream should not be conditioned by the color of a person's skin.

In 1931, in a book entitled *The Epic of America*, James Truslow Adams described the American Dream as the dream of "a land in which life should be better and richer and fuller for every man, with opportunity for each according to his ability or achievement." According to Adams the dream of boundless economic opportunity, accessible to all, has been America's greatest contribution to human history.

Recently, though, there are signs that the U.S. economy is cracking under the strain of high expectations. The stressors that have eroded faith in the American Dream are complex and multifaceted: Globalization has brought with it the outsourcing of jobs to less expensive venues, the declining influence of organized labor, influxes of undocumented immigrant workers, and the U.S. government's apparent unwillingness to enforce its own immigration laws. In addition, rising health-care costs combined with the diminishing availability of health insurance, the growing chasm between chief executive officers' pay and the pay of working people, and a general lack of political and economic leadership are all reasons that have been cited for the declining prospects of American workers.

Whatever the causes, the statistics are difficult to ignore. Between 2001 and 2006, according to Bureau of Labor Statistics data, monthly job growth hovered at an annualized 0.4 percent; the U.S. economy has been creating new jobs more slowly than in any previous period. Workers' real earnings during this time grew by only 1 percent, also much lower than in previous periods, while the cost of food, housing, and household operations has risen slowly but steadily.

Perhaps it is not surprising, then, that consumer indebtedness has also risen. Exactly how much it has risen, however, might be surprising. Average household debt, which equaled roughly 50 percent of household disposable income in the 1950s, was 100 percent of household disposable income in 2002, according to figures published by the Federal Reserve System. Average household debt has continued to rise since 2002, and is currently approaching 130 percent. The inevitable economic consequences of such a huge debt burden became apparent in the late summer of 2007, when mounting numbers of defaults in subprime mortgages—home loans often with escalating interest rates that are offered to borrowers with poor credit histories—set off a crisis that caused credit markets to freeze up for a brief period of time before driving several U.S. lenders out of business and unsettling world financial markets. When large numbers of borrowers are unable to repay their debts, financial institutions can become insolvent, and investors can be left holding the bag.

In August of 2007, in the midst of the subprime lending crisis and perhaps reeling from its impact, the National Association for Business Economics (NABE) reported another surprising fact: The growing inability of Americans to pay their bills is now the biggest concern of its membership, outpacing fear of terrorist attack and concerns about rising gas prices, inflation, and government spending. The greatest source of anxiety among this group of professional economists is that the debt crisis could ultimately lead to higher interest rates, adversely affecting corporate borrowers, which would in turn slow national economic growth and even lead to a recession. In September of 2007, Federal Reserve chairman Ben Bernanke added his voice to the chorus of troubled economists when he warned that the credit market crisis would probably worsen, as many more U.S. homeowners were expected to default on adjustable rate mortgages in the months ahead.

These same fears troubling economists are being mirrored by ordinary Americans. More than 80 percent of U.S. residents now identify household debt as a problem, and 44 percent say they fear being driven into debt as the result of a medical emergency. This is more than the 33 percent who fear being killed or hurt by a terrorist attack, and more than the 38 percent who are concerned they might lose their home in a natural disaster.

Clearly the American Dream has fallen on hard times on a number of different fronts. Some remedies for the credit crisis recommended by NABE members include instituting rules to prevent abusive lending practices, requiring clear language in legal documents, tightening lending standards so that loans are not made to people who do not have the resources to repay them, and increasing financial literacy. Some may argue that these measures, as important as they are, only address a symptom, without getting to the underlying causes of the debt crisis, such as the declining prospects of American workers at all levels of income and education.

Many complex and interrelated factors will shape the future of the U.S. economy. The paralyzing impact of consumer debt is one such factor. The power of the American Dream to motivate and inspire is another. These two are representative of a number of critical concerns that are addressed in *At Issue: The Future of the U.S. Economy.*

The U.S. Economy Is Stronger than Most People Think

David Malpass

David Malpass is the chief economist for Bear Stearns & Co., Inc., a global investment bank.

The United States is the world's biggest producer, exporter, seller, saver, and innovator, and the U.S. economy is strong and growing. This is true in spite of gloomy predictions about the impact of fiscal, trade, and savings deficits. Fear of deficits creates a negative self-image, distorts U.S. participation in trade negotiations, and damages international economic policy. The United States needs to project a confident and dynamic image, and to pursue policies more in keeping with its true financial strength.

The U.S. has a powerful, growing economy, yet we project the "wrong path" image of an aging society drowning in debt and burdening the world with risk. This gloomy fiction distorts our domestic and international economic policymaking. We should reject it and launch a more energetic vision of global prosperity built on economic freedom and dynamism.

Calculated properly, U.S. households have more financial savings—and in most years add more—than the rest of the world combined.

The U.S. is the world's biggest producer, exporter, seller, saver and innovator. On average it adds 30% more to global

GDP [gross domestic product] each year than does all of Asia (45% more in 2006), with one-tenth the population. U.S. employment, wages and profits are at record levels. We're the biggest source of foreign aid and the only major source of its most effective component: private donations.

Despite dire fiscal predictions the federal budget is on a trend that could bring it into balance at the end of the decade, with a debt-to-GDP ratio well below the Clinton Administration's average. Talk of our recklessly low "savings rate" circles the globe yet arbitrarily excludes the economy's trillions of dollars of compound gains. Calculated properly, U.S. households have more financial savings—and in most years add more—than the rest of the world combined.

Fear of fiscal, trade and savings deficits has crippled domestic policymaking.

The loudest hue and cry is over our trade deficit, which is blamed for dragging down our economy, as well as everyone else's. Yet the view that our trade deficit costs jobs and adds to global financial risk can't be reconciled with our 4.5% unemployment rate and the eager flow of long-term, low-cost foreign capital into U.S. investments.

Misreading the U.S. Economy

Fear of fiscal, trade and savings deficits has crippled domestic policymaking. We are in desperate need of tax reform yet believe we "can't afford" it. Both political parties should aggressively lay out their tax visions and invite debate. To have a coherent vision they will first have to reject Washington's stifling assumption that tax reform—no matter how well constructed—doesn't add to economic growth or asset values.

Entitlement reform is also distorted by this mistaken image of U.S. financial collapse. An increase in the Social Security tax burden proposed by austerity advocates would slow the economy without adding one iota of the external funding needed to protect retirees and add to their rate of return. Let's shelve this "reform," which is a disguised tax increase, and instead expand tax-preferred savings vehicles.

As gasoline prices soared in 2005 and 2006, the world held its breath, thinking the U.S. might collapse under the weight of its debt and dependency. Even though the economy survived easily, we are paralyzed by Iran's encroachment into the Strait of Hormuz. We should break this choke hold by offsetting any declines in gasoline prices with an incremental gasoline tax. Naysayers will claim consumers can't afford it, but they already have.

Selling our economy short may be causing even more damage to our international economic policy. In one of the ironies of economics the U.S. apologizes profusely for the global trade imbalance. We accept blame for growing our economy and population faster than our trading partners (which draws in imports) and providing more attractive investments (which brings in foreign capital). Rather, the primary burden should be on the trade-surplus, capital-outflow countries to enhance their economic dimes, not on us to diminish ours.

Cowed by trade-deficit phobia, we require minutely negotiated trade agreements. These are a far cry from the sweeping liberalization that would bring the most benefits to the U.S., the biggest trading nation by far. Trade-policy paralysis insists on agribusiness subsidies and blocks even small reductions in our stiff quotas and duties on the importation of sugar, peanuts, orange juice and ethanol, even though these policies damage the environment and impede growth in developing countries.

Sold Short

The world has huge economic problems. Europe's low birthrate, high unemployment and exodus of human capital are of bigger consequence to the world than the U.S.' deficits, but the latter dominate the G-7's [a group of finance ministers of the seven participating nations of Canada, France, Germany, Italy, Japan, the United Kingdom, and the United States] agenda and world headlines. Japan and South Korea are still relying on corporatism instead of economic flexibility, a global liability as their workforces shrink. The U.S. provides heavy subsidies for large homes and expensive health procedures but lets its infrastructure petrify. Russia's bleak hope is to create energy monopolies fast enough to prevent the Islamic world and China from overrunning its sparsely populated borders. Much of Latin America and Africa are decapitalizing, running IMF-mandated [International Monetary Fund-mandated] fiscal and trade surpluses (capital outflows) that have contributed to their multidecade stagnation in per capita income.

Despite the rich global environment for economic progress, the U.S.—low on self-esteem—has focused on China's yuan as the 21st century's economic scourge. U.S. exports (and global growth) would get a much bigger boost if more countries joined China in growth-promoting currency stability than if China joins them in currency instability. Pleading with China to add to the yuan's value at the dollar's expense parades our weak image and enhances China's strength. At the same time, Latin America seems to have decided the U.S. is one of the weak links in the global economy. It is reaching out to Europe and China for investment and free-trade agreements, with the view that those are the economic relationships of the future. This global misreading of the U.S.' deficits is weakening our friendships and blocking our economic vision, even as our economy enjoys its third decade of robust expansion.

2

The American Dream
Is Slipping Away

David R. Francis

David R. Francis is a writer for the Christian Science Monitor.

U.S. society is becoming more class-bound. In the past, there was a perception that opportunities for success were the almost inevitable result of hard work. Recently, however, it has become more difficult for children to reach beyond the economic prospects of their parents. Lower-income people work hard, yet lose ground financially. Wealth seems to have become a prerequisite for success, with the greatest inequalities affecting women and minorities.

The American dream, at least on the economic side, is fading. Most people see the United States as a special place where there is plenty of opportunity for someone to work hard, play by the rules, and get ahead—maybe even become wealthy.

Today, though, nearly 1 in 5 American households has zero net worth or actually owes more than it owns. And the odds of a son or daughter rising above their parents in such a financial predicament have shrunk.

"Income mobility has declined in the last 20 years," says Bhashkar Mazumder, an economist at the Federal Reserve Bank of Chicago.

What that means is that the US is becoming less of a meritocracy, where skill and intelligence determine success,

David R. Francis, "The American Dream Gains a Harder Edge," *Christian Science Monitor*, May 23, 2005. Reproduced by permission from *Christian Science Monitor* *(www.csmonitor.com)*. www.csmonitor.com/2005/0523/p17s01-cogn.html.

and becoming more of a class-bound society, where economic background, including the better education money can provide, matters more. There are still many rags-to-riches stories. But there's stagnation in the underclass.

There are still many rags-to-riches stories. But there's stagnation in the underclass.

Most Americans don't believe that to be true, surveys show. But academic studies suggest that income mobility in the US is no better than that in France or Britain. It's actually lower than in Canada and is approaching the rigidity of Brazil.

That marks a change from the past.

Perceptions Are Changing

From 1950 to 1980, Americans were more and more likely to see their offspring move up—or down—the income ladder. For example: poor parents in the US had good odds of seeing children make great strides in overcoming their parental heritage. And if they lived long enough, they might well find that a grandchild had risen to a median income level.

Today, it could take five or six generations to close the gap between poverty and middle-class status, calculates Mr. Mazumder.

Of course, there are always exceptions. Remarkable children still get rich—or plunge to the bottom—in one generation, depending on education, attitude, diligence, and other factors. The point is that average intergenerational experience seems to be more frozen in place today.

Of course, Mazumder's research looks at income—not wealth, which results from saving and investing income, and from inheritances.

A broader look at the overall financial security of American families isn't encouraging either. It measures ownership (homes, financial assets, and so on) and protections against financial setbacks, such as health insurance to cover large medical bills that cause almost half of individual bankruptcies.

There are lots of people who have found it difficult to meet their basic needs.

"There are lots of people who have found it difficult to meet their basic needs," says Lillian Woo, an economist in Durham, N.C., with CFED [Council For Economic Development], a national nonprofit research group that conducted the study. "The ratio of indebtedness seems to be growing."

That's not because these Americans have engaged in shopping sprees, though that sometimes happens. It is often because of medical bills or high housing costs. Many households are "hovering on the brink of financial disaster," Ms. Woo maintains. "The cushion is very thin."

For example: 1 in 4 households does not own enough to support itself—even at the poverty line—for three months.

Women and Minorities Suffer Most

The picture is worse for most minorities and women: 1 in 3 minority households has zero net worth or is in debt (compared with the average of 1 in 5). Black families have, on average, only one-sixteenth the net assets of white families. For every dollar of net worth of a household headed by a man, households headed by a woman have less than 40 cents.

The situation also differs widely between states, according to the CFED study. At the top, the median Massachusetts household has more than three times the net worth of median households in Arizona, Texas, Georgia, West Virginia, and a number of other states.

"This issue of net worth and what people owe is important," says Andrea Levere, president of CFED. Her goal for the organization is to widen the opportunities for Americans to build their net worth and ownership position by winning bipartisan support for government programs at the state and federal level.

In the states, CFED supports legislation requiring banks to provide "lifeline bank accounts" to bring more of the poor into mainstream financial services. Some 30 percent of families don't have bank accounts. It wants more states to give better tax breaks, somewhat like the Earned Income Tax Credit of the federal government, to the poor.

It also urges states to ban predatory lenders, who make high-cost loans that can strip the poor of their assets. At present, 29 states have such legislation.

At the federal level, meanwhile, Sens. Rick Santorum (R) of Pennsylvania and Joseph Lieberman (D) of Connecticut have drafted a bill [in 2005] that would provide tax credits for financial institutions that match the savings of low-income customers put into Individual Development Accounts.

But the cost, $1.2 billion, makes its prospects for passage dim in deficit-ridden Washington.

3

Lack of Leadership Is Destroying America's Economic Future

Richard Wolf

Richard Wolf is a reporter for USA Today.

The United States has a broken business model and is struggling with its worst fiscal crisis in years. An aging population, spiraling health-care costs, underfunded retirement accounts, trade imbalances, a burgeoning national debt, and revenue shortfalls all demand leadership, straight talk, real solutions, and decisive action. Yet lawmakers have done nothing to help.

The comptroller general of the United States is explaining over eggs how the nation's finances are going to hell.

"We face a demographic tsunami" that "will never recede," David Walker tells a group of reporters. He runs through a long list of fiscal challenges, led by the imminent retirement of the baby boomers, whose promised Medicare and Social Security benefits will swamp the federal budget in coming decades.

The breakfast conversation remains somber for most of an hour. Then one reporter smiles and asks, "Aren't you depressed in the morning?"

Sadly, it's no laughing matter. To hear Walker, the nation's top auditor, tell it, the United States can be likened to Rome before the fall of the empire. Its financial condition is "worse

Richard Wolf, "A 'Fiscal Hurricane' on the Horizon," *USA Today*, November 14, 2005. Reproduced by permission. www.usatoday.com/news/washington/2005-11-14-fiscal-hurricane-cover_x.htm.

than advertised," he says. It has a "broken business model." It faces deficits in its budget, its balance of payments, its savings—and its leadership.

Deficits Are Out of Control

Walker's not the only one saying it. As Congress and the White House struggle to trim up to $50 billion from the federal budget over five years—just 3% of the $1.6 trillion in deficits projected for that period—budget experts say the nation soon could face its worst fiscal crisis since at least 1983, when Social Security bordered on bankruptcy.

Without major spending cuts, tax increases or both, the national debt will grow more than $3 trillion through 2010, to $11.2 trillion—nearly $38,000 for every man, woman and child.

Without major spending cuts, tax increases or both, the national debt will grow more than $3 trillion through 2010, to $11.2 trillion—nearly $38,000 for every man, woman and child. The interest alone would cost $561 billion in 2010, the same as the Pentagon.

From the political left and right, budget watchdogs are warning of fiscal trouble.

From the political left and right, budget watchdogs are warning of fiscal trouble:

- Douglas Holtz-Eakin, director of the non-partisan Congressional Budget Office [CBO], dispassionately arms 535 members of Congress with his agency's stark projections. Barring action, he admits to being "terrified" about the budget deficit in coming decades. That's when an aging population, health care inflation and advanced medical technology will create a perfect storm of spiraling costs.

- Maya MacGuineas, president of the bipartisan Committee for a Responsible Federal Budget, sees a future of unfunded promises, trade imbalances, too few workers and too many retirees. She envisions a stock market dive, lost assets and a lower standard of living.

- Kent Conrad, a Democratic senator from North Dakota, points to the nation's $7.9 trillion debt, rising by about $600 billion a year. That, he notes, is *before* the baby boom retires. "We're not preparing for what we all know is to come," he says. "We're all sleepwalking through this period."

- Stuart Butler of the conservative Heritage Foundation projects a period from now until 2050 in which tax revenue stays stable as a share of the economy but Medicare, Medicaid and Social Security spending soars. To avoid big tax increases, he says the government has to "renegotiate" the social contracts it made with its citizens.

- Alice Rivlin and Isabel Sawhill of the centrist Brookings Institution put their pessimism into a book titled *Restoring Fiscal Sanity*. Rivlin, who became the first director of the Congressional Budget Office in 1974, says it will take an "economic scare" such as the 1987 stock market crash to spur action. Sawhill likens the growing gulf between what the government spends and takes in to a "Category 6 fiscal hurricane."

A Fiscal Wake-up Tour

They are the preachers of doom and gloom. Liberals and conservatives, Democrats and Republicans, they are trying to be heard above the *ka-ching* of the cash register as it tallies the cost of government benefits and tax cuts, Iraq and Hurricane Katrina. To raise their profile in recent months, several have traveled together to places such as Richmond, Va., and Minneapolis [Minnesota] for what they call a "Fiscal Wake-Up Tour."

Leon Panetta, former White House budget director and chief of staff to President Clinton, calls them "disciples of balanced budgets. . . . And at some point, they'll be proven right."

The White House and Congress are trying to address the nation's short-term budget deficits, but their response pales against the size of the long-term problem.

The White House and Congress are trying to address the nation's short-term budget deficits, but their response pales against the size of the long-term problem. President [George W.] Bush proposed nearly $90 billion in savings over five years in his 2006 budget. He also tried to trim future Social Security benefits for wealthier recipients. The Senate this month [November 2005] approved $35 billion in savings over five years. House Republicans tried to save more than $50 billion last week, but objections from moderates stalled action. Either way, the savings could be wiped out by $70 billion in proposed tax cuts.

The budget-cutting effort is being led by conservatives, who recoiled when Congress quickly voted to spend $62 billion after Hurricane Katrina struck New Orleans and the Gulf Coast [in late August 2005]. "Katrina served as a wake-up call," Walker says.

In prior years, facing a less imminent demographic explosion, Congress cut in politically agonizing increments of $500 billion over five years. Bush's father [George H.W. Bush] gave up his "no new taxes" campaign pledge in 1990. After Ross Perot [the wealthy businessman who ran for president as an Independent] focused attention on the deficit in his 1992 presidential campaign, Clinton and the Democratic-run Congress raised taxes even more in 1993. Clinton and the Republican-run Congress forced two government shutdowns before agreeing on a deficit-reduction package in 1997.

In each case, cutting the deficit backfired at the polls. The elder Bush lost re-election, the Democrats lost Congress, and Republicans' obstinacy helped Clinton win a second term. "The choices you have to make are almost exactly the opposite of what wins political elections," Panetta says.

The problem is also easy for Congress to postpone because the day of reckoning is years away.

The problem is also easy for Congress to postpone because the day of reckoning is years away. This year's [2005] deficit was $319 billion, down $94 billion from the year before. That's 2.6% of the nation's economy, an amount easily borrowed from foreign investors.

A Long List of Problems

But there is every reason to act—and soon. Budget watchdogs cite these looming problems:

- Prescription-drug coverage under Medicare takes effect Jan. 1 [2006]. Its projected cost, advertised at $400 billion over 10 years when it passed in 2003, has risen to at least $720 billion. "We couldn't afford" it, Walker says of the new law.

- The leading edge of the baby boom hits age 62 in 2008 and can take early retirement. The number of people covered by Social Security is expected to grow from 47 million today to 69 million in 2020. By 2030, the Congressional Budget Office projects, Social Security spending as a share of the U.S. economy will rise by 40%.

- The bulk of Bush's 10-year, $1.35 trillion tax-cut program is set to expire at the end of 2010. But Congress is moving to make the reductions permanent. That would keep tax revenue at roughly 18% of the economy, where it's been for the past half-century—too low to support even current spending levels. "We can't afford to make all the tax cuts permanent," Walker says.

• Baby boomers begin to reach age 65 in 2011 and go on Medicare. Of all the nation's fiscal problems, this is by far the biggest. If it grows 1% faster than the economy—a conservative estimate—Medicare would cost $2.6 trillion in 2050, after adjusting for inflation. That's the size of the entire federal budget today.

"Social Security is Grenada," Holtz-Eakin says. "Medicare is Vietnam." [Referring to the two U.S. military conflicts, one being small in scale and short-lived (Grenada) and the other (Vietnam) being long-term, expensive, and unpopular.]

Inaction could have these consequences, experts say: Higher interest rates. Lower wages. Shrinking pensions. Slower economic growth. A lesser standard of living. Higher taxes in the future for today's younger generation. Less savings. More consumption. Plunging stock and bond prices. Recession.

Some veterans of the deficit-cutting wars are pessimistic about avoiding disaster. "In the end, CBO and others are no more than speed bumps on the highway of fiscal irresponsibility," says Robert Reischauer, former Congressional Budget Office director and now president of the non-partisan Urban Institute.

No Easy Answers

The gloom-and-doom crowd hopes to avoid that fate. Increasingly in recent months, they are traveling the country, writing and speaking out about the need to cut spending, raise taxes—or both.

The most outspoken is Walker, an impeccably dressed CPA [certified public accountant] whose 15-year term as head of the Government Accountability Office runs through 2013. He was a conservative Democrat, then a moderate Republican, and is now an independent. He's also a student of history, a Son of the American Revolution who lives on Virginia property once owned by George Washington.

Walker's agency churns out reports with titles such as "Human Capital: Selected Agencies Have Opportunities to Enhance Existing Succession Planning and Management Efforts." But he knows he must try to humanize the numbers, and his rhetoric on the nation's fiscal course has become more acerbic. "Anybody who says you're going to grow your way out of this problem," Walker says, "would probably not pass math."

Holtz-Eakin, a soft-spoken economist who said [in November 2005] . . . he will leave CBO at the end of the year, takes a different approach. Less prone to giving speeches, he sees his role as a consultant and truth-sayer to Congress. "Numbers are the currency of the realm in Washington," he says, and most agree his agency has the best in town. But he concedes, "Sometimes it falls to the consultant to tell the client the bad news."

Holtz-Eakin's father was in steel, a cyclical business rocked by strikes and shutdowns. "I thought, 'This is nuts. No one should live like this,'" he says. That explains why he wants the government to prepare for new demands on its New Deal and Great Society benefit programs. "The baby boom has been getting older one year at a time with a striking regularity," he says.

MacGuineas is the outside agitator. An independent, she worked for Sen. John McCain's presidential campaign in 2000. She respects politicians who deliver bad news, as [Democratic] presidential candidate Walter Mondale did in 1984 when he said tax increases were inevitable—and then was defeated in 49 states.

Asking for Straight Talk

"I want to see a presidential election where the candidates are talking about what taxes they'll raise and what spending they'll cut," she says. "It's not always a winning campaign slogan."

Conrad ran for the Senate in 1986 promising to reduce the budget deficit or quit after six years. By 1992, the deficit had hit an all-time high, and he said he would not seek re-election. Only the death of North Dakota's other senator kept him in Congress.

The former state tax commissioner has been doing this longer than other congressional budget officials—and he has the most charts. He's so numbers-oriented that at baseball games, he can instantly compute a hitter's average after each at-bat. "Numbers speak to me in a way that they don't speak to others," he says. "I guess it's the way my brain is wired."

Sawhill and Butler, from opposite ends of the political spectrum, lead a group of about 15 budget experts at Washington think tanks who gather periodically to discuss their dour crusade. Aided by Walker and the non-partisan Concord Coalition, a fiscal watchdog group, they have taken their show on the road.

Butler, a native of Britain, witnessed there in the 1960s and '70s the effects of slow growth and high unemployment, driven partly by generous government benefits. "We have a responsibility" to start the debate, he says, "because we don't have to get re-elected." But Sawhill says it's "an indictment of our political leadership that it is being left to outside groups such as ours to put these issues on the agenda."

After three decades in the business, Rivlin is frustrated by lawmakers' inaction and blames balanced-budget advocates for not better articulating the problem. "There may be better ways to talk about it," she says. "I sometimes think, 'Where's Ross Perot when we need him?'"

4

Growing Income Inequality in the U.S. Is Not a Sign of a Weak Economy

Gary S. Becker and Kevin M. Murphy

Gary S. Becker and Kevin M. Murphy are fellows at the Hoover Institution at Stanford University and members of the faculty at the University of Chicago. Becker won the Nobel Prize in Economics in 1992 and Murphy was the 1997 winner of the John Bates Clark Medal of the American Economic Association.

Income inequality in the United States has become a growing concern. This inequality, however, is the result of greater investments in education and the acquisition of advanced skills by American workers and should not be considered a sign of economic weakness. The education-linked wage gap is found in all racial groups and among men and women alike. Higher education and skill levels benefit the broader economy as well as individuals, resulting in rising wages, greater productivity, and better living standards.

Income inequality in China substantially widened, particularly between households in the city and the countryside, after China began its rapid rate of economic development around 1980. The average urban resident now makes 3.2 times as much as the average rural resident, and among city dwellers alone, the top 10 percent makes 9.2 times as much as the bottom 10 percent. But at the same time that inequality rose, the number of Chinese who live in poverty fell—from 260 million in 1978 to 42 million in 1998. Despite the widening gap in incomes, rapid economic development dramatically improved the lives of China's poor.

In the United States, the rise in inequality accompanied a rise in the payoff to education and other skills.

Politicians and many others in the United States have recently grown concerned that earnings inequality has increased among Americans. But as the example of China—or India, for that matter—illustrates, the rise in inequality does not occur in a vacuum. In the case of China and India, the rise in inequality came along with an acceleration of economic growth that raised the standard of living for both the rich and the poor. In the United States, the rise in inequality accompanied a rise in the payoff to education and other skills. We believe that the rise in returns on investments in human capital is beneficial and desirable, and policies designed to deal with inequality must take account of its cause.

Just as in China and India, this growing inequality gap is associated with growing opportunity—in this case, the opportunity to advance through education.

A Highly Educated Workforce Makes a Difference

To show the importance to inequality of the increased return to human capital, consider the link between earnings and education. . . . In 1980, an American with a college degree earned about 30 percent more than an American who stopped education at high school. But, in recent years, a person with a college education earned roughly 70 percent more. Meanwhile, the premium for having a graduate degree increased from roughly 50 percent in 1980 to well over 100 percent today. The labor market is placing a greater emphasis on education, dispensing rapidly rising rewards to those who stay in school the longest.

This trend has contributed significantly to the growth in overall earnings inequality in the United States. And just as in China and India, this growing inequality gap is associated with growing opportunity—in this case, the opportunity to advance through education. The upward trend in the returns to education is not limited to one segment of the population. Education premiums for women and African Americans have increased as much as, or more than, the premiums for all workers.

The growth in returns to education for women has paralleled that for men over the past 25 years, but has remained at a somewhat higher level. Returns for blacks have increased as much as those for whites. The potential to improve one's labor-market prospects through higher education is greater now than at any time in the recent past, and this potential extends across gender and racial lines.

The growth in returns to college has generated a predictable response: as the education earnings gap increased, a larger fraction of high school graduates went on to college. The proportion of men and women ages 20 to 25 who attended college jumped by about half over the past 40 years, tracking the rise in the wage premium. When returns fell in the 1970s, the fraction going on to college declined. The rise in returns since 1980 has been accompanied by a significant rise in the fraction going on to college.

This increase in the proportion of persons going on to higher education is found among all racial and ethnic groups, but it is particularly important for women, who, in 2004, outnumbered men as students in degree-granting institutions of higher education by 33 percent.

Women have also shifted toward higher-earnings fields, such as business, law, and medicine: the number of women in graduate schools rose 66 percent between 1994 and 2004, while the number of men rose just 25 percent. And the greater education achievement of women compared to men is particularly prominent among blacks and Latinos: the proportion of black women who attend colleges and universities jumped from 24 percent to 43 percent between 1974 and 2003, while the proportion of white men rose only from 41 percent to 49 percent.

The potential generated by higher returns to education extends from individuals to the economy as a whole.

Education Pays Off

The potential generated by higher returns to education extends from individuals to the economy as a whole. Growth in the education level of the population has been a significant source of rising wages, productivity, and living standards over the past century. Higher returns to education will accelerate growth in living standards as existing investments have a higher return, and additional investments in education will be made in response to the higher returns. Gains from the higher returns will not be limited to GDP [gross domestic product] and other measures of economic activity; education provides a wide range of benefits not captured in GDP, and these will grow more rapidly as well due to the additional investments in schooling.

Why is the earnings gap widening? Because the demand for educated and other skilled persons is growing.

Why is the earnings gap widening? Because the demand for educated and other skilled persons is growing. That is hardly surprising, given developments in computers and the Internet, advances in biotechnology, and a general shift in economic activity to more education-intensive sectors, such as finance and professional services. Also, globalization has encouraged the importing of products using relatively low-skilled labor from abroad. At the same time, world demand has risen for the kinds of products and services that are provided by high-skilled employees.

When calculating the returns to education, we look at the *costs* of education as well. And even accounting for the rise in university tuition (it more than doubled, on average, in constant dollars between 1980 and 2005), overall returns to college and graduate study have increased substantially. Indeed, it appears that the increases in tuition were partly induced by the greater return to college education. Pablo Peña, in a Ph.D. dissertation in progress at the University of Chicago, argues convincingly that tuition rose in part because students want to invest more in the quality of their education, and increased spending per student by colleges is partly financed by higher tuition levels. More investment in the quality and quantity of schooling will benefit both individuals and society.

Should an increase in earnings inequality due primarily to higher rates of return on education and other skills be considered a favorable rather than an unfavorable development? We think so.

Inequality Is Not a Negative Thing

This brings us to our punch line. Should an increase in earnings inequality due primarily to higher rates of return on education and other skills be considered a favorable rather than an unfavorable development? We think so. Higher rates of return on capital are a sign of greater productivity in the economy, and that inference is fully applicable to human capital as well as to physical capital. The initial impact of higher returns to human capital is wider inequality in earnings (the same as the initial effect of higher returns on physical capital), but that impact becomes more muted and may be reversed over time as young men and women invest more in their human capital.

We conclude that the forces raising earnings inequality in the United States are beneficial to the extent that they reflect higher returns to investments in education and other human capital. Yet this conclusion should not produce complacency, for the response so far to these higher returns has been disturbingly limited. For example, why haven't more high school graduates gone on to a college education when the benefits are so apparent? Why don't more of those who go to college finish a four-year degree? (Only about half do so.) And why has the proportion of American youth who drop out of high school, especially African-American and Hispanic males, remained fairly constant?

The answers to these and related questions lie partly in the breakdown of the American family, and the resulting low skill levels acquired by many children in elementary and secondary school—particularly individuals from broken households. Cognitive skills tend to get developed at very early ages while, as our colleague James Heckman has shown, noncognitive skills—such as study habits, getting to appointments on time, and attitudes toward work—get fixed at later, although still relatively young, ages. Most high school dropouts certainly appear to be seriously deficient in the noncognitive skills that would enable them to take advantage of the higher rates of return to education and other human capital.

So instead of lamenting the increased earnings gap caused by education, policymakers and the public should focus attention on how to raise the fraction of American youth who complete high school and then go on for a college education. Solutions are not cheap or easy. But it will be a disaster if the focus remains so much on the earnings inequality itself that

Congress tries to interfere directly with this inequality rather than trying to raise the education levels of those who are now being left behind.

For many, the solution to an increase in inequality is to make the tax structure more progressive—raise taxes on high-income households and reduce taxes on low-income households. While this may sound sensible, it is not. Would these same individuals advocate a tax on going to college and a subsidy for dropping out of high school in response to the increased importance of education? We think not. Yet shifting the tax structure has exactly this effect.

A more sensible policy is to try to take greater advantage of the opportunities afforded by the higher returns to human capital and encourage more human capital investment. Attempts to raise taxes and impose other penalties on the higher earnings that come from greater skills could greatly reduce the productivity of the world's leading economy by discouraging investments in its most productive and precious form of capital—human capital.

5

Childhood Poverty Weakens the U.S. Economy

Harry J. Holzer

Harry Holzer is a professor of public policy at Georgetown University, and a visiting fellow at the Urban Institute in Washington, D.C.

Many people argue from moral grounds that childhood poverty should be reduced. However, there are also economic arguments for ending childhood poverty. Children raised in poverty have lower lifetime earnings. They are more likely to engage in crime and to suffer from poor health. Based on these proven negative outcomes, it is good policy for the government to invest in universal prekindergarten programs, to expand the Earned Income Tax Credit for the working poor, and to provide job training and other cost-effective measures to reduce poverty.

$\displaystyle M$r. Chairman,

Thank you for inviting me to speak today on the economic costs of poverty to the United States.

I'd like to share with all of you some recent findings of a paper I coauthored with several colleagues for the Task Force on Poverty of the Center for American Progress. The paper attempts to estimate the economic costs of child poverty in the U.S.

Most arguments for reducing poverty in the U.S., especially among children, rest on a *moral* case for doing so—one

Harry J. Holzer testimony, Hearing on the Economic and Societal Costs of Poverty, House Ways and Means Committee, January 24, 2007. www.americanprogress.org/iss ues/2007/01/holzer_testimony.html.

that emphasizes the unfairness of child poverty, and how it runs counter to our national creed of equal opportunity for all.

But there is also an *economic* case for reducing child poverty. When children grow up in poverty, they are more likely as adults to have low earnings, which in turn reflect low productivity in the workforce. They are also more likely to engage in crime and to have poor health later in life. Their reduced productive activity generates a direct loss of goods and services to the U.S. economy. Any crime in which they engage imposes large monetary and other personal costs on their victims, as well as the costs to the taxpayer of administering our huge criminal justice system. And their poor health generates illness and early mortality that requires large healthcare expenditures, impedes productivity and ultimately reduces their quality and quantity of life.

Most arguments for reducing poverty in the U.S., especially among children, rest on a moral case for doing so.

In each case, we reviewed a range of rigorous research studies that estimate the average statistical relationships between growing up in poverty, on the one hand; and one's earnings, propensity to commit crime and quality of health later in life, on the other. We also reviewed estimates of the costs that crime and poor health per person impose on the economy. Then we aggregated all of these average costs per poor child across the total number of children growing up in poverty in the U.S. to estimate the aggregate costs of child poverty to the U.S. economy. We had to make a number of critical assumptions about how to define and measure poverty, what level of income to use as a non-poverty benchmark, and which effects are really caused by growing up in poverty and not simply correlated with it. Wherever possible, we made conservative assumptions, in order to generate lower-bound estimates.

Our results suggest that the costs to the U.S. associated with childhood poverty total about $500 billion per year, or the equivalent of nearly 4 percent of GDP [gross domestic product].

The Economic Case for Reducing Childhood Poverty

Our results suggest that the costs to the U.S. associated with childhood poverty total about $500B per year, or the equivalent of nearly 4 percent of GDP [gross domestic product]. More specifically, we estimate that childhood poverty each year:

- Reduces productivity and economic output by about 1.3 percent of GDP;

- Raises the costs of crime by 1.3 percent of GDP; and

- Raises health expenditures and reduces the value of health by 1.2 percent of GDP.

If anything, these estimates almost certainly understate the true costs of poverty to the U.S. economy. For one thing, they omit the costs associated with poor adults who did not grow up poor as children. They ignore all other costs that poverty might impose on the nation besides those associated with low productivity, crime and health—such as environmental costs, and much of the suffering of the poor themselves.

What does all of this imply for public policy? The high cost of childhood poverty to the U.S. suggests that investing significant resources in poverty reduction might be more cost-effective over time than we previously thought. Of course, determining the effectiveness of various policies requires careful evaluation research in a variety of areas. But a range of policies—such as universal pre-kindergarten (or pre-K) programs, various school reform efforts, expansions of the Earned Income Tax Credit (EITC) and other income supports for the working poor, job training for poor adults, higher minimum wages and more collective bargaining, low-income neighborhood revitalization and housing mobility, marriage promotion, and faith-based initiatives—might all be potentially involved in this effort. Given the strong evidence that already exists on some of these efforts (like high-quality pre-K and the EITC), some investments through these mechanisms seem particularly warranted.

At a minimum, the costs of poverty imply that we should work hard to identify cost-effective strategies of poverty remediation, and we should not hesitate to invest significant resources when these strategies are identified. In the meantime, we should also experiment with and evaluate a wide range of promising efforts.

6

Free Trade Is Good for the U.S. Economy

Robert Krol

Robert Krol is a professor of economics at California State University at Northridge.

Although the Constitution gives Congress the power to regulate trade, Congress transferred this power to the president in the aftermath of the Great Depression. This gave the president greater flexibility and more credibility with representatives of other countries. Free trade contributes an estimated ten thousand dollars to average household income in the United States and would contribute even more if all remaining trade barriers were eliminated. While it is true that trade agreements have disadvantaged some workers in the short term by depressing wages and reducing job opportunities, wage insurance is one way to offset these effects.

The dramatic expansion of trade over the last quarter of a century has raised America's standard of living. This doesn't mean everyone is better off, however. In the short run, some American workers have lost jobs. Media pundits like Lou Dobbs often play up the job losses and ignore the many benefits of trade. This kind of populist coverage can turn public opinion against freer trade.

Congress must soon decide whether it will renew the President's Trade Promotion Authority which gives the President the ability to negotiate reductions in trade barriers. How-

Robert Krol, "How to Help Those Harmed by Trade Agreements," *TCS Daily*, May 23, 2007. Reproduced by permission. www.tcsdaily.com/printArticle.aspx?ID=052307A.

ever, the Democratic-controlled Congress is likely to be pressured by unions and other groups that oppose freer trade to withhold the authority. Succumbing to these pressures would be costly to this country. With the right program in place, it would also be unnecessary.

Expanding the existing wage insurance program can offset some of the costs to displaced workers. An expanded and less bureaucratic wage insurance program would offer displaced workers help, yet avoid the negative employment effects of traditional programs aimed at the unemployed. This approach would allow the majority of Americans to benefit from expanded trade and effectively help those who are harmed.

Researchers . . . estimate that since World War II, free trade gets credit for raising the average household income in the U.S. by $10,000.

The Benefits of Trade

Under the U.S. Constitution, Congress has the power to regulate trade. In 1934, faced with the disastrous economic consequences of protectionist policies during the Great Depression, Congress transferred the power to negotiate trade policy to the President. The President would negotiate trade deals and Congress would give the proposed agreement a simple up or down vote. By prohibiting Congressional power to modify an agreement, this transfer of power gave executive branch negotiators flexibility and credibility with representatives of other countries. Foreign negotiators could make concessions without fearing further demands would be placed on them when the agreement reached Congress.

The resulting liberalization of trade has made a tremendous contribution to America's economic well being. Researchers at the Institute for International Economics in Washington D.C. estimate that since World War II, free trade gets credit

39

for raising the average household income in the U.S. by $10,000. The U.S. Office of the Trade Representative estimates that about $2,000 of the income gain can be attributed to the North American Free Trade Agreement and multilateral tariff reductions during the early 1990s. The Institute estimates that the elimination of all remaining trade barriers would raise household income in the United States by another $5,000.

International trade raises a country's standard of living in a number of ways. Consumers and businesses can buy products and services at lower prices. This is a boost in real income, especially important to middle and lower income families. Not only are the items we buy cheaper, there is far greater variety. U.S. businesses can choose between the best domestic and foreign produced machinery for their factories. Competition from imports forces domestic firms to clean up their act and improve efficiency in order to turn a profit. Finally, new ideas are imbedded in the items we buy from the rest of the world. This can help accelerate productivity growth at home.

A challenge for Congress, as it renews the Trade Promotion Authority, is to pick effective policies that help those adversely affected by trade.

How to Help Those Harmed

Although the overall economic gains from trading with the world are large, not everyone is made better off. Skills-based technological change has generally improved job opportunities and wages in the U.S. (the U.S. economy has generated 1.5 million jobs a year since the early 1990s, net of job loss), but trade has depressed wages and reduced job opportunities for some less-skilled workers. Given the substantial benefits of trade over time, it makes sense to continue to expand trade and to offset the negative consequences with policies aimed at helping displaced workers. Not all strategies are equally good.

A challenge for Congress, as it renews the Trade Promotion Authority, is to pick effective policies that help those adversely affected by trade.

Experience tells us that the government may be able to help in job placement, but government job training efforts have not been particularly successful. Extended unemployment compensation eases the short-term economic damage of a lost job, but has the negative effect of discouraging people from looking for jobs, keeping them out of the labor force way too long. The more effective strategy would be to expand the federal wage insurance program that was part of the 2002 Trade Act.

Wage insurance provides older displaced workers who accept a lower paying job a government payment equal to one-half the difference between the old wage and the new wage. The program lasts for up to two years and has a $10,000 cap on total payments.

Wage insurance has an advantage over other policies designed to aid displaced workers. First, unlike unemployment insurance, it creates an incentive to get back into the workforce promptly. The longer a worker remains unemployed, the harder it is to find a job. A worker may start at a lower wage but, with experience, wages increase over time. Second, the on-the-job training workers receive by getting back into the labor market is far more effective in creating marketable skills than government-run job training programs.

The United States is a major exporter and importer of manufactured goods. The President's Trade Promotion Authority has played a key role in expanding trade. Congress should renew the Trade Promotion Authority and expand the wage insurance program to offset the costs to those displaced workers faced with less attractive job prospects.

U.S. Trade Policy Has Hurt the Manufacturing Sector

Alan Tonelson and Peter Kim

Alan Tonelson and Peter Kim conduct research for the U.S. Business & Industry Council.

Many people are aware of the impact of foreign imports on the U.S. automotive industry. What is less well known is that other U.S. manufacturing sectors also have suffered due to foreign imports. By 2005 imports represented between 50 and 59 percent of overall U.S. sales of manufactured goods. Much of this loss of market share can be attributed to failed international trade policies, including the North American Free Trade Agreement (NAFTA), which encouraged manufacturers to build plants in foreign countries.

It's been all over the news: Imports have helped decimate the U.S.-owned automotive industry. What hasn't been as widely reported, though, is that literally dozens of other U.S.-based manufacturing industries are suffering similar losses in their home market. The bottom line, as revealed in a new study by the U.S. Business & Industry Council: While the United States remains a military superpower, it is steadily becoming an industrial has-been.

U.S. Manufacturing Keeps Losing Ground

The council's survey of import levels in domestic manufacturing shows that 111 of 114 key U.S.-based industries lost domestic market share to foreign-produced goods between 1997

Alan Tonelson and Peter Kim, "U.S. Losing Ground, Even in the U.S.," *Plastics News*, vol. 18, February 5, 2007. Used with permission of Plastics News. Copyright © 2007. All rights reserved.

and 2005. From 2004–05 alone, import penetration rose for 83 of these sectors and fell for just 31.

In many cases, imports have made stunningly rapid inroads into critical U.S. manufacturing markets.

These industries, moreover, are exclusively the kinds of high-value, capital-intensive sectors, like aircraft engines and wireless communications gear, that make up the backbone of any world-class national manufacturing base. Lower-value, labor-intensive sectors that were long ago overwhelmed by foreign competition, like apparel, toys, and low-end consumer electronics, were left out of the study.

In many cases, imports have made stunningly rapid inroads into critical U.S. manufacturing markets. Between 1997 and 2005, 26 of the 114 industries saw their home market share shrink by 50 percent or more, including pharmaceuticals; computers; telecommunications hardware; navigation and guidance equipment; broadcasting and wireless communications equipment; and motor vehicle power train and transmission equipment.

Eight more sectors experienced market-share losses of nearly 50 percent to imports during this period, notably tires; switch-gear and switchboard apparatus; and commercial and service industry machinery.

As a result, by 2005, imports represented at least 50–59 percent of sales in the United States in 24 of the 114 industries studied, including telecommunications hardware; heavy-duty trucks and chassis; and broadcast and wireless communications gear.

In eight more industries, imports have captured 60–69 percent of the U.S. market, including autos, environmental controls and aircraft engines and engine parts. And in six sectors, imports control 70 percent or more of the American market, including machine tools. If current trends continue, imports will account for the majority of U.S. domestic sales in sectors such as electricity measuring and test equipment; X-ray equipment; turbines and turbine generator sets; laboratory instruments; and construction machinery.

Rising import penetration means that U.S.-based producers are flunking the most important test of competitiveness—winning and keeping customers. Just as revealing, surging imports are already replacing and depressing U.S. production throughout domestic manufacturing.

Between 1997 and 2005, output actually fell in nearly two-thirds of the 53 industries where import penetration is highest or grew fastest, and stagnated in many of the rest.

These losses at home are especially worrisome because the American market is the arena in which U.S.-based manufacturers should do best. After all, they should be most familiar with local tastes, and they face no trade barriers at home. If domestic industry can't even defend its home turf, how can it hope to compete abroad?

High-Tech Losses

The import-penetration data also show that American manufacturing's woes even extend to the high-tech sector, supposedly the nation's best hope for future prosperity and an area of natural advantage for the United States. Yet some of the biggest recent losers of home market share include such technology pillars as semiconductor production equipment, electricity measuring and test equipment (critical for all high-tech manufacturing), telecommunications hardware, navigation and guidance devices, and pharmaceuticals.

Why such dismal results for such important U.S. industries? Two major failures of U.S. international trade policy bear much of the blame. First, Washington has done a terrible job of combating the numerous predatory trade policies, ranging from currency manipulation to illegal subsidies, pursued by other major trading powers to gain industrial supremacy.

Second, too many U.S. trade pacts since the North American Free Trade Agreement have encouraged American-owned multinational companies to supply U.S. markets by moving abroad—and thus literally to build powerful manufacturing bases in foreign countries.

The core manufacturing sectors suffering these mounting losses at home have traditionally led the U.S. economy in productivity and innovation, and have generated America's best-paying jobs on average. They also undergird the nation's security. But if imports' growing domination of American industrial markets is not reversed soon, scores of these critical industries could get pushed past the point of no return.

8

Foreign Investment Is Good for the U.S. Economy

Tim Kane

Tim Kane is director of the Center for International Trade and Economics at the Heritage Foundation.

Large U.S. trade deficits have drawn criticism from some policy makers. However, trade deficits are not dangerous to the economy when they are counterbalanced by a surplus of investments from abroad. This is the case: While the U.S. trade deficit is $63.9 billion, more than $9 trillion in U.S. assets are owned by foreign investors. Policy makers need to be wary of addressing the trade deficit by regulating capital markets in ways that inconvenience foreigners who seek to do business in the United States, as these policies may inadvertently destroy American jobs.

On May 10 [2007] Treasury Secretary Hank Paulson led a small panel discussion about the importance of foreign direct investment in the American economy. Just a few hours earlier, a government report was released showing a trade deficit of $63.9 billion in March, nearly 10 percent higher than in February. The trade deficit is a favorite bogeyman of those who predict a coming economic apocalypse, so the latest figures are certain to be much cited. The coincidence of the trade figures and the Paulson panel just might goad policymakers to focus on the real economic issue in play. Trade "imbalances" in goods and services pose no danger as long as

Tim Kane, "Are Foreign Trade and Investment Unbalanced?" *Heritage Foundation Web Memo*, May 14, 2007, copyright © 2007 the Heritage Foundation. Reproduced by permission. www.heritage.org/Research/Economy/upload/wm_1455.pdf.

they are counterbalanced by a surplus of investment. Fortunately, the U.S. enjoys exactly such a surplus. The potential danger, then, is radical policy changes that would worsen the investment climate. Investors need certainty, and uncertainty is a growing concern, according to Paulson's panel.

A Trade Surplus with Free Economies

Total March [2007] exports were $126.2 billion, or barely two-thirds of the $190.1 billion in total imports, according to the U.S. Bureau of Economic Analysis. The result was a trade deficit $6.0 billion larger than in February.

By country, the U.S. had the largest trade *surpluses* with Hong Kong ($1.3 billion), Australia ($1.3 billion), and Singapore ($0.9 billion). The largest trade deficits in March were with China ($17.2 billion, compared to $18.4 billion in February), Europe ($8.9 billion, compared to $7.2 billion in February), OPEC [Organization of Petroleum Exporting Countries] ($8.9 billion, compared to $7.0 billion in February), Japan ($7.1 billion), and Mexico ($6.7 billion).

Notably, the top three largest U.S. trade surpluses came from the *2007 Index of Economic Freedom*'s three freest countries: Hong Kong, Singapore, and Australia. This indicates that the United States can compete in a more liberalized trading environment. The other implication is that trade restrictions in less free economies are hindering exports from the U.S.

The good news is that exports are still growing, up $1.8 billion for goods in March to $90.2 billion. Services exports grew $0.4 billion to $36.1 billion, primarily in financial, insurance, and technical/professional services.

Imports grew even faster, which may seem counter-intuitive given the weaker exchange rate. However, the combination of long-term contracts and a short-term dollar decline inevitably leads to a short-term widening of the trade gap before it narrows, which is known as the "J-Curve." Imports of goods alone increased $7.8 billion in March. But this should turn around if the dollar stabilizes.

Investment Clouds

Two decades ago, investors from Japan famously snapped up American movie studios, manufacturers, and even famous properties like the Rockefeller Center. Foreign investors were also eager to get in on the ground floor of the Internet revolution and participated heavily in private equity deals in U.S. startups during the late 1990s. According to the Council of Economic Advisors, "U.S. affiliates owned $5.5 trillion in assets and had $2.3 trillion in sales." Foreign multinational employment accounts for 4.7 percent of all U.S. jobs, and those jobs pay $15,200 more, on average, than purely domestic jobs.

America enjoys a healthy stock of foreign investment from abroad and continues to enjoy a very large flow of new inbound investments.

A useful framework for thinking about economic issues is to identify differences between levels and changes, or "stock" versus "flow." For example, a nation may have no stock of fresh water but receive a regular flow of thousands of gallons from rains. America enjoys a healthy stock of foreign investment from abroad and continues to enjoy a very large flow of new inbound investments. But there is a qualitative difference in the two.

Foreign investors own a total stock of over $9 trillion in U.S. assets, according to 2005 CEA [Council of Economic Advisors] data. The assets are composed of four basic types, and the largest portion is foreign direct investment (FDI, $2.8 trillion). This type of investment goes directly into companies and infrastructure and, so, is considered the best in terms of creating high-value jobs for U.S. workers. Inward FDI is more stable and less liquid than other sorts of capital inflows, demonstrating long-term foreign investor confidence in the U.S. economy. U.S.-based multinational companies, a key source of FDI, also contribute to the U.S. economy by exposing domestic firms to the best business management techniques.

The other three types of foreign investment are corporate stocks, private bonds, and U.S. Treasury bonds and bills. Each of these types comprises about $2 trillion of the total investment stock.

But the stock is only part of the story, because it includes investments that have accumulated over decades, even centuries. What about the flow of investments in recent years? Professor Menzie Chin, an economist at the University of Wisconsin, writes that the U.S. has become overly reliant on bond financing and that FDI has been drying up significantly. In the last five years, only one in 10 dollars invested in the U.S. has been in FDI, while eight have been in bonds. This is a cause of concern.

If investors lose faith in the investment process, including things like cumbersome approval rules and strict travel restrictions, then they will react, often by investing elsewhere. The visa waiver issue in particular has become a point of contention for America's friends. One investor reaction has been a shift toward passive investments in the U.S., which are much more liquid. The danger is that if the demand for passive investments flags, U.S. interest rates will rise.

The policy implication for Congress is to tread very carefully in regulating capital markets and playing politics with the international economy. The Dubai Ports World imbroglio [complicated situation] was nothing short of a fiasco in terms of the signal it sent to foreign investors. Ongoing saber rattling about exchange rates and punitive tariffs may seem to be harmless rhetoric, but it has an impact. American legislators who are talking tough do not intend to scare away good jobs, but that appears to be the result.

9

An Immigrant Workforce
Is Good for America

Daniel Griswold

Daniel Griswold is director of the Center for Trade Policy Studies at the Cato Institute.

Critics of comprehensive immigration reform complain that increased social welfare costs for migrant labor are an unfair burden on taxpayers. However, studies of the economic impact of immigrant workers show that the cost to American society is more than balanced by the workers' positive contributions. The best response to fiscal concerns about immigration is not to suppress labor migration, but to control and reallocate government spending to support health care and education rather than welfare programs.

One frequently heard criticism of comprehensive immigration reform is that it will prove too costly to taxpayers. The mostly low-skilled workers who would be admitted and legalized under the leading reform plan now being considered by the U.S. Congress would typically pay fewer taxes than native-born Americans and presumably consume more means-tested welfare services. Critics of reform argue that legalizing several million undocumented workers and allowing hundreds of thousands of new workers to enter legally each year will ultimately cost American taxpayers billions of dollars.

One recent study from the Heritage Foundation, for example, claims that each "low-skilled household" (one headed

Daniel Griswold, "The Fiscal Impact of Immigration Reform: The Real Story," *Center for Trade Policy Studies*, May 21, 2007. Copyright © 2007 CATO Institute. Reproduced by permission. www.freetrade.org/node/667.

by a high-school dropout) costs federal taxpayers $22,000 a year. Spread out over 50 years of expected work, the lifetime cost of such a family balloons to $1.1 million. If immigration reform increases the number of such households in the United States, it will allegedly cost U.S. taxpayers several billion dollars a year.

It is certainly true that low-skilled workers do, on average, consume more in government services than they pay in taxes, especially at the state and local levels. But some of the estimates of that cost have been grossly exaggerated. Moreover, the value of an immigrant to American society should not be judged solely on his or her fiscal impact.

The Real Fiscal Impact of Immigration

The wilder estimates of the fiscal impact of low-skilled immigrants are contradicted by more credible estimates. In May 2006 the Congressional Budget Office [CBO] calculated that the 2006 Comprehensive Immigration Reform Act (S. 2611) then before the U.S. Senate would have a positive impact of $12 billion on the federal budget during the decade after passage. The 2006 legislation, like current proposals, would have allowed low-skilled foreign-born workers to enter the United States through a temporary worker program, and it would have allowed several million undocumented workers in the United States to obtain legal status.

Specifically, the CBO estimated that federal spending would increase $53.6 billion during the period 2007–16 if the legislation became law, primarily because of increases in refundable tax credits and Medicaid spending. The additional spending would be more than offset in the same period by an even greater increase in federal revenues of $65.7 billion, mostly due to higher collections of income and Social Security taxes but also because of increased visa fees.

One frequently cited figure on the cost of low-skilled immigrants comes from the authoritative 1997 National Research

Council study, *The New Americans: Economic, Demographic, and Fiscal Effects of Immigration.* The study calculated the lifetime fiscal impact of immigrants with different educational levels. The study expressed the impact in terms of net present value (NPV), that is, the cumulative impact in future years expressed in today's dollars. The study estimated the lifetime fiscal impact of a typical immigrant without a high school education to be a negative NPV of $89,000. That figure is often cited by skeptics of immigration reform.

The children of immigrants typically outperform their parents in terms of educational achievement and income.

What is less often considered is that the NRC study also measured the fiscal impact of the descendants of immigrants. That gives a much more accurate picture of the fiscal impact of low-skilled immigrants. It would be misleading, for example, to count the costs of educating the children of an immigrant without considering the future taxes paid by the educated children once they have grown and entered the workforce. The children of immigrants typically outperform their parents in terms of educational achievement and income. As a result, the NRC calculated that the descendants of a typical low-skilled immigrant have a positive $76,000 fiscal impact, reducing the net present value of the fiscal impact of a low-skilled immigrant and descendants to $13,000.

Even that figure does not give the full picture. As the NRC study was being written, Congress passed the 1996 Personal Responsibility and Work Opportunity Reconciliation Act, otherwise know as the 1996 Welfare Reform Act. The act contains an entire title devoted to restricting immigrant access to means-tested welfare, limiting access of noncitizens to such public benefit programs as food stamps and Medicaid. When the NRC study accounted for the impact of the 1996 Welfare

Reform Act, the fiscal impact of a single low-skilled immigrant and descendants was further reduced to $5,000 in terms of net present value.

If we accept the NRC estimates, then allowing an additional 400,000 low-skilled immigrants to enter the United States each year would have a one-time NPV impact on federal taxpayers of $2 billion. That cost, while not trivial, would need to be compared to the efficiency gains to the U.S. economy from a larger and more diverse supply of workers and a wider range of more affordable goods and services for native-born Americans. In a post–September 11 [2001] security environment, comprehensive immigration reform could also reduce federal spending now dedicated to apprehending illegal economic immigrants.

The Impact on Roads, Schools, Hospitals, and Crime

Increased immigration has also been blamed for crowded roads, hospitals, public schools, and prisons. In all four of those cases, the negative impact of immigration has been exaggerated.

As for congestion of roads, immigration has played a secondary role in population growth nationally and at a more local level. Nationally, net international migration accounts for 43 percent of America's annual population growth, with natural growth still accounting for a majority of the growth. On a local level, an analysis of U.S. Census data shows that, for a typical U.S. county, net international migration accounted for 28 percent of population growth between 2000 and 2006. Natural growth from births over deaths accounted for 38 percent of growth on a county level and migration from other counties 34 percent. One-third of U.S. counties actually lost population between 2000 and 2006 as birthrates continue to fall and Americans migrate internally to the most economically dynamic metropolitan areas. If local roads seem more crowded, it is not typically immigration but natural growth and internal migration that are mostly responsible.

As for alleged overcrowding at public schools, low-skilled immigrants cannot be singled out for blame. Enrollment in the public school system has actually been declining relative to the size of America's overall population. The share of our population in K-12 [kindergarten through twelfth grade] public schools has fallen sharply in recent decades, from 22 percent of the U.S. population in 1970 to 16 percent today. As with roads, overcrowding in certain school districts is more likely to be driven by new births and internal migration than by newly arrived immigrants.

"Even as the undocumented population has doubled since 1994, the violent crime rate in the United States has declined 34.2 percent and the property crime rate has fallen 26.4 percent."

As for crime and the inmate population, again, immigration is not the major driver. Indeed, the violent crime rate in the United States has actually been trending down in recent years as immigration has been increasing. After rising steadily from the 1960s through the early 1990s, the rate of violent crime in the United States dropped from 758 offenses per 100,000 population in 1991 to 469 offenses in 2005. As a recent study by the Immigration Policy Center [IPC] concluded,

Immigrants are less likely to be jailed than are their native-born counterparts with similar education and ethnic background. The same IPC study found that "for every ethnic group without exception, incarceration rates among young men are lowest for immigrants, even those who are least educated." Other studies reveal that immigrants are less prone to crime, not because they fear deportation, but because of more complex social factors. All the available evidence contradicts the misplaced fear that allowing additional low-skilled immigrants to enter the United States will somehow increase crime and incarceration rates.

Low-skilled immigrants tend to under-use health care because they are typically young and relatively healthy.

As for hospitals, especially emergency rooms, the presence of uninsured, low-skilled workers in a particular area does impose additional costs on hospitals in the form of uncompensated care. There is no evidence, however, that illegal immigration is the principal cause of such costs nationwide. Indeed, low-skilled immigrants tend to underuse health care because they are typically young and relatively healthy.

A recent report from the Rand Corporation found that immigrants to the United States use relatively few health services. The report estimates that all levels of government in the United States spend $1.1 billion a year on health care for undocumented workers aged 18 to 64. That compares to a total of $88 billion in government funds spent on health care for all adults in the same age group. In other words, while illegal immigrants account for about 5 percent of the workforce, they account for 1.2 percent of spending on public health care for all working-age Americans.

Low-skilled immigrants allow important sectors of the U.S. economy, such as retail, cleaning, food preparation, construction, and other services, to expand to meet the needs of their customers.

The Impact on State and Local Governments

Although the fiscal impact of low-skilled immigrants has been exaggerated by opponents of reform, it can impose real burdens at a local level, particularly where immigration inflows are especially heavy. The 1997 National Research Council study found that, although the fiscal impact of a typical immigrant and his or her descendants is strongly positive at the federal level, it is negative at the state and local level.

State and local fiscal costs, while real, must be weighed against the equally real and positive effect of immigration on the overall economy. Low-skilled immigrants allow important sectors of the U.S. economy, such as retail, cleaning, food preparation, construction, and other services, to expand to meet the needs of their customers. They help the economy produce a wider array of more affordably priced goods and services, raising the real wages of most Americans. By filling gaps in the U.S. labor market, such immigrants create investment opportunities and employment for native-born Americans. Immigrants are also consumers, increasing demand for American-made goods and services.

Several state-level studies have found that the increased economic activity created by lower-skilled, mostly Hispanic immigrants far exceeds the costs to state and local governments. A 2006 study by the Kenan Institute of Private Enterprise at the University of North Carolina at Chapel Hill found that the rapidly growing population of Hispanics in the state, many of them undocumented immigrants, had indeed imposed a net cost on the state government of $61 million, but the study also found that those same residents had increased the state's economy by $9 billion.

A 2006 study by the Texas comptroller of public accounts reached a similar conclusion. Examining the specific fiscal impact of the state's 1.4 million undocumented immigrants, the study found that they imposed a net fiscal cost on Texas state and local governments of $504 million in 2005. The fiscal cost, however, was dwarfed by the estimated positive impact on the state's economy of $17.7 billion.

The Right Policy Response

The right policy response to the fiscal concerns about immigration is not to artificially suppress labor migration but to control and reallocate government spending. The 1996 Welfare Reform Act was a step in the right direction. It recognized that welfare spending was undermining the longterm interests of low-income households in the United States, whether native-born or immigrant, by discouraging productive activity. The law led to a dramatic decrease in the use of several major means-tested welfare programs by native-born and immigrant households alike. Further restrictions on access to welfare for temporary and newly legalized foreign-born workers would be appropriate.

The federal government could compensate state and local governments that are bearing especially heavy up-front costs due to the increase in low-skilled immigration.

Another appropriate policy response would be some form of revenue sharing from the federal to state and local governments. The federal government could compensate state and local governments that are bearing especially heavy up-front costs due to the increase in low-skilled immigration. The transfers could offset additional costs for emergency room health care services and additional public school enrollment. Such a program would not create any new programs or additional government spending; it would simply reallocate government revenues in a way that more closely matched related spending.

Misplaced apprehensions about the fiscal impact of immigration do not negate the compelling arguments for comprehensive immigration reform, nor do they justify calls for more spending on failed efforts to enforce our current dysfunctional immigration law. If the primary goal is to control the size of government spending, then Congress and the president should seek to wall off the welfare state, not our country.

10

Better Wage Insurance Would Provide a Safety Net for American Workers

Lael Brainard

Lael Brainard is vice president and founding director of the Global Economy and Development Program at the Brookings Institution. She served as deputy national economic adviser and chair of the Deputy Secretaries Committee on International Economics during the Clinton administration.

Globalization and technological change are among the primary reasons why growing numbers of American workers are experiencing economic insecurity. Employees leave jobs more often than in years past, and workers who are involuntarily displaced often accept subsequent work at a lower rate of pay than their previous jobs. Income insurance, health insurance, and retraining programs need to be strengthened. Wage insurance is important because it encourages workers to consider a wider range of employment options and it provides a cushion against losses in income that may be unavoidable. It should be available to all permanently displaced workers who have had at least two years of tenure in their previous position.

Chairman [George] Miller, Congressman [Howard P. "Buck"] McKeon, members of the Committee, I appreciate the opportunity to testify before your committee today.

Lael Brainard, House Committee on Education and Labor Hearing, March 26, 2007. www.brookings.edu/testimony/2007/0326labor_brainard.aspx.

59

Today's Economic Realities

American workers today face a very different employment outlook than their parents encountered back in the 1960s— when Trade Adjustment Assistance was enacted under President John F. Kennedy.

With increased turnover and increased competition come increased uncertainty and, for some workers, increased economic insecurity.

Today's workers are much more likely to transition several times between different employers over the course of their working lifetimes. According to Princeton scholar Henry Farber, men currently in the age range of 35 to 64 are almost 20 percentage points less likely to be in ten-year jobs as were males in this age range roughly 45 years ago.

Today, a much larger expanse of occupations and sectors are exposed to the bracing winds of global competition—with trade now exceeding 25 percent of national income compared with less than 10 percent back in the 1960s.

The data suggest inequality is once again on the rise in many of the world's richer economies.

With increased turnover and increased competition come increased uncertainty and, for some workers, increased economic insecurity. For permanently displaced workers who suffer earnings losses, average earnings in the new job are 16 percent lower than earnings in the previous job, while displaced manufacturing workers moving into lower paying jobs face an average 20 percent drop in earnings. The consequences of job loss are particularly damaging in import-competing industries, where displaced workers face longer spells of unemployment and greater permanent wage declines than do workers in other industries.

The causes for increased insecurity faced by American middle class households are complex, but almost certainly include globalization and changes in technology among the primary drivers. The current episode of global integration dwarfs previous expansions: the entry of India and China into the global labor force amounts to an expansion of roughly 70 percent—concentrated at the lower end of the wage scale. Textbook economics would predict a squeeze on wage earners until capital and technology investments adjust. And the data suggest inequality is once again on the rise in many of the world's richer economies.

Because China is successfully pursuing at a scale never seen before a growth strategy that is export-led and foreign direct investment fed, its rise is sending waves to the farthest reaches of the global economy. China is already deeply embedded in global manufacturing supply chains, confronting higher wage manufacturers with the difficult choice of moving up the value chain or lowering costs.

India's concurrent economic emergence has complicated the challenge. While India is pursuing a growth strategy more reliant on domestic consumption and investment than China, nonetheless its success in exporting higher skilled "knowledge" services such as software programming has expanded the scope of globalization. Many Americans in white collar occupations are confronting the reality of low wage foreign competition for the first time.

An ever-broader pool of American workers is finding that the nation's safety net has more holes than netting.

How Effective Are Existing Programs?

Today's [March 26, 2007] hearing addresses the question, "How Effective are Existing Programs in Helping Workers Impacted by International Trade?" The answer is simple: existing programs are not nearly as effective as they must be in helping workers who may face the prospect of large earnings declines as well as loss of health insurance when their jobs are displaced through no fault of their own. In the face of accelerated job losses in manufacturing and white-collar offshoring in services, an ever-broader pool of American workers is finding that the nation's safety net has more holes than netting.

Despite the fact that the U.S. labor market ranks second to none when it comes to job turnover, the nation's safety net for easing job transitions remains one of the weakest among the wealthy economies. In comparison with other high income countries, not only do U.S. unemployment benefits have a shorter duration, but displaced workers in America face the prospect of losing health benefits along with income. The main federally mandated unemployment insurance (UI) program contains so many restrictions that today only about 40 percent of all jobless workers receive benefits.

The last serious overhaul of the nation's employment safety net was in 1962, when President John F. Kennedy established the TAA program to compensate workers who suffer job loss as a result of trade liberalization. But workers have long found it difficult, time-consuming, and expensive to prove that they are entitled to extended unemployment benefits under the nation's Trade Adjustment Assistance (TAA) program.

In 2002 Congress overhauled and expanded TAA, adding a health care tax credit, doubling the training budget, and substantially raising budget outlays for income support. But the TAA program continues to disappoint. Participation has remained surprisingly low, thanks in part to confusing Department of Labor interpretations and practices that ultimately deny benefits to roughly three-quarters of workers who are certified as eligible for them. TAA has helped fewer than 75,000 new workers per year, while denying more than 40 percent of all employers' petitions. And remarkably, the Department of Labor has interpreted the TAA statute as excluding the growing number of services workers displaced by trade.

Despite its laudable goals, the TAA program has repeatedly failed to meet expectations. Between 2001 and 2004, an average of only 64 percent of participants found jobs while they participated in TAA. And earnings on the new job were more than 20 percent below those prior to displacement.

Expanding Training and Insurance While Unemployed

I believe we have a brief window of opportunity to align the nation's policies against the new economic realities facing American families. In the first instance, this means instituting a set of policies that support good jobs and good pay here in America. They range from investing in education and workforce training to infrastructure and competitiveness policies.

But we should also seize on this window of opportunity to strengthen the nation's safety net to better insure against the economic insecurity faced by too many American families. That means strengthening the income and health insurance available to workers during periods of unemployment, broadening access and improving the quality of retraining programs, and insuring against sharp earnings losses once reemployed. Let me be clear about this: I think all three elements are not only compatible with each other but essential.

Strengthening income and health insurance and retraining programs while workers are unemployed are absolutely essential—but not sufficient when workers too often face the prospect of much lower earnings even after they secure a job following permanent displacement. Let's take trade displaced workers as an example. For those displaced workers who qualify for TAA, even after taking advantage of the extended unemployment benefits and relatively expansive training benefits that are available under TAA, earnings in their new jobs are on average 20 percent below their old jobs.

The evidence on earnings losses following permanent displacement is sufficiently compelling to warrant a serious examination of additional policy instruments to help workers once they are reemployed—not just while they are unemployed. The time has come to augment existing programs by adopting a new insurance program that insures against sharp declines in wages, not just unemployment, for permanently displaced workers.

A chief goal of wage insurance is to smooth the incomes of workers who suffer permanent displacement and declines in their earnings.

A chief goal of wage insurance is to smooth the incomes of workers who suffer permanent displacement and declines in their earnings. Wage insurance is most likely to have overall positive economic benefits if it targets workers whose earnings would otherwise fall dramatically as forces outside their control devalue their skills.

Evidence suggests that wage insurance encourages workers to consider different types of jobs and sectors of employment and, therefore, broadens the job search.

Evidence suggests that wage insurance encourages workers to consider different types of jobs and sectors of employment and, therefore, broadens the job search. This is particularly important for displaced workers whose firm-specific skills have declined in value. And wage insurance can facilitate valuable on-the-job training; the training that a displaced worker receives on a new job provides new skills that contribute directly to his or her performance in the new job.

By replacing some of the lost earnings, wage insurance could also encourage more rapid reemployment; a Canadian pilot wage insurance program reduced unemployment durations by 4.4 percent on average.

Because the goal is to provide partial insurance against extreme income fluctuations, wage insurance should be available to all permanently displaced workers, who have at least two years of tenure at the previous job. It might also make sense to restrict the program to workers displaced from full-time jobs and reemployed full-time, so as to avoid any possible incentive to reduce hours of work. Further, the compensation period would be limited to some transition period, perhaps 2 years, long enough to help strengthen the new employment relationship.

The wage loss replacement rate, the duration of benefits, and the annual cap on compensation determine the kinds of workers who would benefit most from the program. A high replacement rate (such as 70 percent) combined with a low annual compensation cap would provide the greatest cushion to lower-income workers suffering steep losses in earnings, while a lower replacement rate (such as 30 percent) combined with a high annual cap would tilt benefits toward higher income earners.

According to our estimates, a wage insurance program that replaces 50 percent of earnings losses for long tenure full-time displaced workers up to a maximum of $10,000 per year for up to two years would cost roughly $3.5 billion per year, assuming modest offsetting savings in other programs. On a per worker basis, this cost falls midway between the current unemployment and retraining benefits available under UI and Worker Investment Act (WIA) programs and the comprehensive cost of TAA benefits.

How do we think about the price tag? The net cost of $3.5 billion per year amounts to an insurance premium of roughly $25 per worker per year.

Under such a program, an average trade-displaced worker, who earned $37,382 in 2004 and was reemployed with a 26 percent loss rate at $27,662 would instead receive $33,522 for the first two years after reemployment, thus enabling them to smooth their income while becoming more valuable in the new job.

Of course, the costs can be substantially reduced by offering more modest benefits. For a high-unemployment year such as 2003, costs could range from a low of $1.6 billion for a one-year program with a 30 percent replacement rate and a $10,000 cap to a high of $7 billion for a two-year program with a 70 percent replacement rate and a $20,000 annual cap.

Wage insurance could provide an important tool—in a broader set of policies—designed to help American middle class families insure against disruptive income fluctuations, while preserving the benefits of a dynamic economy. For the price of $25 per worker per year, wage insurance could be an important policy tool to help make work pay following displacement. Faced with a unique window of opportunity to finally make progress in updating and strengthening America's fraying safety net, it would be a shame not to move forward boldly on all fronts to provide greater economic security to American families.

11

The Future Is Bleak for U.S. Workers

Paul Craig Roberts

Paul Craig Roberts was the assistant secretary of the treasury in the Ronald Reagan administration. He was associate editor of the Wall Street Journal *editorial page and contributing editor of* National Review.

Forbes.com, the U.S. Chamber of Commerce, the George W. Bush administration, and many corporations have attempted to paint an optimistic picture of job growth in the United States. The numbers tell a different story, however: of the millions of outsourced jobs and of the H-1B visas issued to hundreds of thousands of foreign workers while American workers languish in the ranks of the unemployed. The United States is the first country in history to destroy the prospects and the living standards of its own workforce. The resulting polarization of rich and poor will lead to political instability and social strife.

On February 20 [2006] Forbes.com told its readers with a straight face that "the American job-generation machine rolls on. The economy will create 19 million new payroll jobs in the decade to 2014." Forbes took its information from the 10-year jobs projections from the Bureau of Labor Statistics [BLS], US Department of Labor, released last December [2005].

If the job growth of the past half-decade is a guide, the forecast of 19 million new jobs is optimistic, to say the least.

Paul Craig Roberts, "America's Bleak Jobs Future," *CounterPunch*, March 6, 2006. Reproduced by permission. www.counterpunch.org/roberts03062006.html.

According to the Bureau of Labor Statistics payroll jobs data, from January 2001–January 2006 the US economy created 1,054,000 net new private sector jobs and 1,039,000 net new government jobs for a total five-year figure of 2,093,000. How does the US Department of Labor get from 2 million jobs in five years to 19 million in ten years?

I cannot answer that question.

No sign of these jobs can be found in the payroll jobs data. But there is abundant evidence of the lost American jobs.

The Truth Is in the Numbers

However, the jobs record for the past five years tells a clear story. The BLS payroll jobs data contradict the hype from business organizations, such as the US Chamber of Commerce, and from "studies" financed by outsourcing corporations that offshore jobs outsourcing is good for America. Large corporations, which have individually dismissed thousands of their US employees and replaced them with foreigners, claim that jobs outsourcing allows them to save money that can be used to hire more Americans. The corporations and the business organizations are very successful in placing this disinformation in the media. The lie is repeated everywhere and has become a mantra among no-think economists and politicians. However, no sign of these jobs can be found in the payroll jobs data. But there is abundant evidence of the lost American jobs.

Information technology workers and computer software engineers have been especially heavily hit by offshore jobs outsourcing. [From January 2001 to January 2006] the information sector of the US economy lost 645,000 jobs or 17.4% of its work force. Computer systems design and related [fields] lost 116,000 jobs or 8.7% of its work force. Clearly, jobs outsourcing is not creating jobs in computer engineering and information technology [IT]. Indeed, jobs outsourcing is not even creating jobs in related fields.

For the past five years US job growth was limited to these four areas: education and health services, state and local government, leisure and hospitality, financial services. There was no US job growth outside these four areas of domestic nontradable services.

Oracle, for example, which has been handing out thousands of pink slips, has recently announced two thousand more jobs being moved to India. How is Oracle's move of US jobs to India creating jobs in the US for waitresses and bartenders, hospital orderlies, state and local government and credit agencies, the only areas of job growth?

Engineering jobs in general are in decline, because the manufacturing sectors that employ engineers are in decline. During the last five years, the US work force lost 1.2 million jobs in the manufacture of machinery, computers, electronics, semiconductors, communication equipment, electrical equipment, motor vehicles and transportation equipment. The BLS payroll job numbers show a total of 70,000 jobs created in all fields of architecture and engineering, including clerical personnel, over the past five years. That comes to a mere 14,000 jobs per year (including clerical workers). What is the annual graduating class in engineering and architecture? How is there a shortage of engineers when more graduate than can be employed?

Of course, many new graduates take jobs opened by retirements. We would have to know the retirement rates to get a solid handle on the fate of new graduates. But it cannot be very pleasant, with declining employment in the manufacturing sectors that employ engineers and a minimum of 65,000 H-1B visas annually for foreigners [nonimmigrants skilled in a "specialty occupation"] plus an indeterminate number of L-1 visas [for nonimmigrants to work for a relatively short time period].

Not content with outsourcing Americans' jobs, corporations want to fill the remaining jobs in America with foreigners on work visas.

Corporations Bypass U.S. Workers

It is not only the [George W.] Bush regime that bases its policies on lies. Not content with outsourcing Americans' jobs, corporations want to fill the remaining jobs in America with foreigners on work visas. Business organizations lie about a shortage of engineers, scientists and even nurses. Business organizations have successfully used public relations firms and bought-and-paid-for "economic studies" to convince policymakers that American business cannot function without H-1B visas that permit the importation of indentured employees from abroad who are paid less than the going US salaries. The so-called shortage is, in fact, a replacement of American employees with foreign employees, with the soon-to-be-discharged American employee first required to train his replacement.

It is amazing to see free-market economists rush to the defense of H-1B visas. The visas are nothing but a subsidy to US companies at the expense of US citizens.

Keep in mind this subsidy to US corporations for employing foreign workers in place of Americans as we examine the Labor Department's projections of the ten fastest growing US occupations over the 2004–2014 decade.

All of the occupations with the largest projected employment growth (in terms of the number of jobs) over the next decade are in nontradable domestic services. The top ten sources of the most jobs in "superpower" America are: retail salespersons, registered nurses, postsecondary teachers, customer service representatives, janitors and cleaners, waiters and waitresses, food preparation (includes fast food), home health aides, nursing aides, orderlies and attendants, general and operations managers. Note that none of this projected employment growth will contribute one nickel toward producing goods and services that could be exported to help close the massive US trade deficit. Note, also, that few of these jobs classifications require a college education.

Among the fastest growing occupations (in terms of rate of growth), seven of the ten are in health care and social assistance. The three remaining fields are: network systems and data analysis with 126,000 jobs projected or 12,600 per year; computer software engineering applications with 222,000 jobs projected or 22,200 per year, and computer software engineering systems software with 146,000 jobs projected or 14,600 per year.

Assuming these projections are realized, how many of the computer engineering and network systems jobs will go to Americans? Not many, considering the 65,000 H-1B visas each year (650,000 over the decade) and the loss during the past five years of 761,000 jobs in the information sector and computer systems design and related [fields].

Judging from its ten-year jobs projections, the U.S. Department of Labor does not expect to see any significant high-tech job growth in the U.S.

Judging from its ten-year jobs projections, the US Department of Labor does not expect to see any significant high-tech job growth in the US. The knowledge jobs are being outsourced even more rapidly than the manufacturing jobs were. The so-called "new economy" was just another hoax perpetrated on the American people.

Facts Are Being Suppressed

If offshore jobs outsourcing is good for US employment, why won't the US Department of Commerce release the 200-page, $335,000 study of the impact of the offshoring of US high-tech jobs? Republican political appointees reduced the 200-page report to 12 pages of public relations hype and refuse to allow the Technology Administration experts who wrote the report to testify before Congress. Democrats on the House Science Committee are unable to pry the study out of the hands of Commerce Secretary Carlos Gutierrez. Obviously, the facts don't fit the Bush regime's globalization hype.

CnnMoney.com reported that America's large financial institutions are moving "large portions of their investment banking operations abroad."

The only thing America has left is finance, and now that is moving abroad. [Recently] CNNMoney.com reported that America's large financial institutions are moving "large portions of their investment banking operations abroad." No longer limited to back-office work, offshoring is now killing American jobs in research and analytic operations, foreign exchange trades and highly complicated credit derivatives contracts. Deal-making responsibility itself may eventually move abroad. [The auditing firm of] Deloitte Touche says that the financial services industry will move 20 percent of its total costs base offshore by the end of 2010. As the costs are lower in India, that will represent more than 20 percent of the business. A job on Wall St. is a declining option for bright young persons with high stress tolerance.

The BLS payroll data that we have been examining tracks employment by industry classification. This is not the same thing as occupational classification. For example, companies in almost every industry and area of business employ people in computer-related occupations. A recent study from the Association for Computing Machinery claims: "Despite all the publicity in the United States about jobs being lost to India and China, the size of the IT employment market in the United States today is higher than it was at the height of the dot.com boom [of the late 1990s]. Information technology appears as though it will be a growth area at least for the coming decade."

We can check this claim by turning to the BLS Occupational Employment Statistics. We will look at "computer and mathematical employment" and "architecture and engineering employment."

Computer and mathematical employment includes such fields as "software engineers applications," "software engineers systems software," "computer programmers," "network systems and data communications," and "mathematicians." Has this occupation been a source of job growth?

Declining Numbers in Many Fields

In November of 2000 this occupation employed 2,932,810 people. In November of 2004 (the latest data available), this occupation employed 2,932,790, or 20 people fewer. Employment in this field has been stagnant for the past four years.

During these four years, there have been employment shifts within the various fields of this occupation. For example, employment of computer programmers declined by 134,630, while employment of software engineers applications rose by 65,080, and employment of software engineers systems software rose by 59,600. (These shifts might merely reflect change in job or occupation title from programmer to software engineer.)

These figures do not tell us whether any gain in software engineering jobs went to Americans. According to [University of California, Davis, computer science] Professor Norm Matloff, in 2002 there were 463,000 computer-related H-1B visa holders in the US. Similarly, the 134,630 lost computer programming Jobs (if not merely a job title change) may have been outsourced offshore to foreign affiliates.

Architecture and engineering employment includes all the architecture and engineering fields except software engineering. The total employment of architects and engineers in the US declined by 120,700 between November 1999 and November 2004. Employment declined by 189,940 between November 2000 and November 2004, and by 103,390 between November 2001 and November 2004.

Clearly, engineering and computer-related employment in the US has not been growing, whether measured by industry or by occupation.

There are variations among fields. Between November 2000 and November 2004, for example, US employment of electrical engineers fell by 15,280. Employment of computer hardware engineers rose by 15,990 (possibly these are job title reclassifications). Overall, however, over 100,000 engineering jobs were lost. We do not know how many of the lost jobs were outsourced offshore to foreign affiliates or how many of any increase in computer hardware jobs went to foreign holders of H-1B or L-1 visas.

Moreover, with a half million or more foreigners in the US on work visas, the overall employment numbers do not represent employment of Americans. Perhaps what corporations and "studies" mean when they claim offshore outsourcing increases US employment is that the contacts companies make abroad allow them to bring in more foreigners on work visas to displace their American employees.

American employees have been abandoned by American corporations and by their representatives in Congress. America remains a land of opportunity—but for foreigners—not for the native born. A country whose work force is concentrated in domestic nontradable services has no need for scientists and engineers and no need for universities. Even the projected jobs in nursing and school teachers can be filled by foreigners on H-1B visas.

In the US the myth has been firmly established that the jobs that the US is outsourcing offshore are being replaced with better jobs. There is no sign of these jobs in the payroll jobs data or in the occupational statistics. Myself and others have pointed out that when a country loses entry level jobs, it has no one to promote to senior level jobs. We have also pointed out that when manufacturing leaves, so does engineering, design, research and development, and innovation itself.

On February 16 [2006] the *New York Times* reported on a new study presented to the National Academies that concludes that outsourcing is climbing the skills ladder. A survey of 200 multinational corporations representing 15 industries in the US and Europe found that 38 percent planned to change substantially the worldwide distribution of their research and development work, sending it to India and China. According to the *New York Times*, "More companies in the survey said they planned to decrease research and development employment in the United States and Europe than planned to increase employment."

The study and discussion it provoked came to untenable remedies. Many believe that a primary reason for the shift of R&D to India and China is the erosion of scientific prowess in the US due to lack of math and science proficiency of American students and their reluctance to pursue careers in science and engineering. This belief begs the question why students would chase after careers that are being outsourced abroad.

The main author of the study, Georgia Tech professor Marie Thursby, believes that American science and engineering depend on having "an environment that fosters the development of a high-quality work force and productive collaboration between corporations and universities." The Dean of

Engineering at the University of California, Berkeley, thinks the answer is to recruit the top people in China and India and bring them to Berkeley. No one seems to understand that research, development, design, and innovation take place in countries where things are made. The loss of manufacturing means ultimately the loss of engineering and science. The newest plants embody the latest technology. If these plants are abroad, that is where the cutting edge resides.

The United States is the first country in history to destroy the prospects and living standards of its labor force.

The United States is the first country in history to destroy the prospects and living standards of its labor force. It is amazing to watch freedom-loving libertarians and free-market economists serve as full time apologists for the dismantling of the ladders of upward mobility that made the America of old an opportunity society.

America has begun a polarization into rich and poor. The resulting political instability and social strife will be terrible.

12

A National Health-Care Plan Would Strengthen the U.S. Economy

Susan Froetschel

Susan Froetschel is assistant editor for YaleGlobal Online.

The U.S. auto industry is losing ground in the global economy, partly because of the lack of a low cost, universal health-care plan for American workers. Private health-care costs have destroyed the profitability of the U.S. automakers. Among top auto-producing nations, only the United States and China do not provide universal coverage. If the United States fails to address this problem and reduce the cost of health care for all Americans, it will risk destroying its industrial economy.

Turmoil in the US auto industry continues to grab headlines, most recently with rumor of a merger between two giants, General Motors [GM] and Chrysler. Whether that comes to pass or not, the US automobile industry that once helped ensure the nation's domination of world manufacturing has become exhibit A for the ill effects of globalization.

A closer look reveals how the industry's declining profits and rising layoffs are a product of both global competition and failure of domestic reform. Nations cannot insulate domestic policies from globalization's cost-cutting pressure, and the US must endure painful alignment with global trends in non-trade issues like health care.

Times Have Changed

Since the launch of the Model T by Henry Ford in the early 20th century, the US has been the world's largest maker of cars. But no more. To reduce costs, the auto industry led all US sectors with job reductions in 2006—more than 150,000 in all. The major firms will close more than 15 plants by 2010. Japan's Toyota could bump General Motors from its perch as the world's leading automaker this year [2007].

Such woes stem from US resistance to two global trends: the drive toward fuel efficiency and universal health coverage. US fuel prices, among the lowest in the world, discouraged the design of smaller cars, and post–WWII [post–World War II] prosperity discouraged Americans from embracing less costly national health care.

Toyota and other firms that offer fuel-efficient vehicles gain market shares with every spike in the price of oil—starting with the OPEC [Organization of Petroleum Exporting Countries] embargo in 1973 and more recently with growing Asian demand. Imports now hold about 40 percent of the US market. Yet US firms would stall without global trade: GM has captured the top spot in the Chinese market, and US firms save money by using parts made in Asia.

By purchasing parts made overseas, US manufacturers avoid high labor costs at home. It also means laying off thousands of workers who produced those parts. One reason behind the high labor costs: The US stands alone among developed nations with its lack of a government-funded health program that reins in costs.

Of the six auto-producing nations, only the US and China do not provide universal coverage.

Of the top six auto-producing nations, only the US and China do not provide universal coverage. Since 1950, the US counted on businesses to provide health-insurance coverage to both workers and their families—no burden during post-war boom years.

In contrast, Japan has required membership in national or employee insurance programs since 1961: Individuals pay about 20 percent of their medical costs up to a ceiling, after which full coverage is provided. Only China has a higher percentage of private expenditures than that of the US: About half of China's urban workers are insured and pay up to 50 percent of costs; most rural workers are uninsured, paying for care with saved or borrowed funds. Or they go without.

In response to low wages overseas, US firms move jobs abroad and reduce health-care benefits at home.

The High Cost of Health Care

Health care raises the price of each GM car by $1,500, complains CEO [chief executive officer] Rick Wagoner. That figure, bandied about by the media, is unsound for several reasons. The calculation overlooks government subsidies: Tax subsidies for employee-sponsored health-care coverage on active workers exceeded $200 billion in 2006, reports the US Internal Revenue Service.

GM's own policy analysts divorce themselves from the figure because health-care costs per car vary, depending on which parts, from light bulbs to seat covers, are outsourced.

With every plant closure, health care costs per car rise because US firms carry an extra burden of coverage for retired workers.

Besides, with every plant closure, health-care costs per car rise because US firms carry an extra burden of coverage for retired workers. GM covered health care for 1.1 million people in 2005, almost 70 percent of whom were retirees or workers' family members.

To regain some competitive edge, the executives want autoworkers to accept cuts in health benefits or the Democratic majority in Congress to reduce health-care costs. Medical care has long served as a hot issue for Democrats, who express concern about the growing numbers of uninsured, now 15 percent of the US population.

A shrinking majority of Americans, now 59 percent, hold employer-provided coverage. Voters demand more health care, so the issue appears intractable. In 1994, President Bill Clinton couldn't convince another Democratic-controlled Congress to consider a health-care reform package, proposed by a task force led by Hillary Clinton, then first lady, now senator for New York and a presidential candidate.

The government picks up the health-care tab for the poor and elderly. Yet, US health care is a powerful industry that generates profits and donates funds to politicians who propose expanded services rather than painful cuts. Between 1998 and 2005, the pharmaceutical and insurance industries ranked first and second in lobbying expenditures, according to the Center for Responsive Politics. Lobbies representing pharmaceutical and insurance industries, hospitals and health-care professionals combined spent more than $2 billion for the period.

Health-care and social-service workers now outnumber manufacturing employees, according to US Census data. Consequently, bringing US health spending in line with that of emerging manufacturing nations is difficult to achieve.

An Unsustainable Situation

It's not just the health of the auto industry that hinges on reducing health costs. A system that spends almost $2 trillion annually on health care is unsustainable as long as patients demand first-class treatment while expecting someone else—government or employers—to pay for it.

States have unveiled plans to tax businesses that do not offer health insurance and require citizens to purchase coverage, and the [George W.] Bush administration proposes complex changes in the tax code. But the piecemeal approach only creates loopholes and leads to more deterioration in US competitiveness.

A government-funded system of basic care could increase US competitiveness by decreasing administrative and other costs and emphasizing prevention.

Americans can no longer afford indulging in more health-care spending per capita than other top nations that manufacture autos—Japan, Germany, China, South Korea and France.

The economics of US health care are not hopeless. A once-dominant manufacturing industry can be reinvigorated.

A government-funded system of basic care could increase US competitiveness by decreasing administrative and other costs and emphasizing prevention. Individuals and companies could purchase extra insurance for private care. Reform could guarantee basic care for all citizens. Incentives could limit an obsession with quick fixes, both in medical treatment and policies.

One way or another, Americans must reduce health care costs—or risk killing the industrial golden goose that has provided so much prosperity.

Government regulation could allow US auto-manufacturers to focus on product innovation rather than health care. Firms like Toyota and Tata of India scramble to design small cars for developing nations—costing as little as $2500. To keep up, US industry must adapt products to a limited supply of energy combined with increasing global demand.

US auto manufacturers want a national health-care plan, suggests Michael Stanton, president of the Association of International Automobile Manufacturers, with confidence.

Bruce Bradley, director of General Motors health-care strategy and policy, denies the existence of any silver bullet, yet notes that government is the largest purchaser of health care and, with industry, can "have an impact on the provider community."

One way or the other, Americans must reduce health-care costs—or risk killing the industrial golden goose that has provided so much prosperity. Globalization, which delivers low inflation and low-priced consumer goods, requires US industry to invest in both health-care reform and innovative designs for a changing market. Or else, the US will lose any hope of a competitive edge in a borderless market.

13

Employer-Mandated Health Care Will Hurt the Economy

Jot Condie

Jot Condie is president and chief executive of the California Restaurant Association.

Health-care reform promises to be an issue in the 2008 presidential election. A bill passed by the California state assembly in 2003 would have levied $7 billion a year in taxes to create a state-run health-care system, placing an unbearable burden on employers, schools, local governments, and charities. Luckily, a coalition was formed to defeat the measure. The restaurant industry is now waging a similar battle against health-care reform, because it is economically impossible for the restaurant industry to assume the skyrocketing costs of health insurance for its employees.

Voters still are recovering from the last election, and already more than a dozen candidates are climbing into the 2008 presidential ring. Campaign speeches, vague promises and character assassination begin to fill the air.

So why should the restaurant industry care this early in the game?

A growing anti-business movement is in high gear, with an ever-increasing number of policies hostile to business finding their way into state legislatures and onto Election Day ballots.

Jot Condie, "Critical Condition: Industry Must Stop the Spread of Unfair Health Care Reform," *Nation's Restaurant News*, April 9, 2007. Reprinted by permission. www.nrn.com/.

Already, health care reform has emerged as a premier domestic issue. Presidential aspirants have made it a top priority in their campaigns, and legislators and activists have continued to highlight access and costs of health care.

How serious is this issue to restaurateurs? The California Restaurant Association [CRA] has been engaged in the fight over health care reform for nearly five years. In 2003, the state Assembly passed aggressive legislation to require all employers in the state with 20 or more employees to provide full medical insurance for their employees.

The costs of this measure would have been staggering—a $7 billion annual tax on employers, schools, local government and charities to create a government-run state health care system. Thousands of Californians would have lost their jobs. We predicted the employer requirement would have driven about 20 percent of our members out of business.

We formed a coalition called Californians Against Government Run Health Care to overturn this measure, labeled Proposition 72. While the CRA was an opponent of the measure, our opposition was not to universal health care, but to the idea that employers should bear most of the costs to fund a societal goal that would benefit all Californians, working or not.

A Battle Worth Fighting

It was a hard-fought battle that came down to the wire: an enormous effort in dollars and labor between the signature-gathering process, countless legal battles, the air war on television and boots on the ground. By the fall we were armed with a sizable war chest, a compelling message and virtually every major newspaper editorial board in our corner.

Ultimately, we were able to convince voters after they learned about the damaging impacts of the initiative. On Election Day, we very narrowly defeated the measure. The cost for maintaining the status quo? Forty million dollars. We raised and spent about half of that. Proponents of Proposition 72 accounted for the other half.

In the following years, Proposition 72-style proposals became the centerpiece of the debate on health care. Today, we are seeing multiple legislative proposals and activist-driven efforts to put employer mandated health care on the ballot in multiple states.

Some would have you believe that there are good employers who offer health care and bad employers who do not. In reality, it is the double-digit increases in health care premiums that divide California employers into those who can afford the out-of-control costs and those who cannot.

Last January [2007], Gov. Arnold Schwarzenegger announced a new plan for California that includes a mandate requiring employers to spend up to 4 percent of their payrolls on health care. Other California legislators have proposed similar legislation, bringing the number of proposals to six.

Four of the legislative plans so far have an employer mandate, yet don't address the true problem: cost.

They all speak of shared responsibility, but most contain burdensome employer mandates targeting California small businesses. A disproportionate burden will fall on small, labor-intensive businesses in low-margin, entry-level wage industries such as restaurants, compared with high-margin, very profitable businesses such as law firms. The more employees a business has relative to income, the greater the economic burden becomes when measured as a percentage of payroll. The greatest sacrifice will come from those businesses least able to pay.

Fifteen additional state legislatures have introduced bills calling for employer mandates to provide health insurance. If passed, you may have no choice but to cut labor costs by reducing employee hours, overtime or eliminating other benefits. Worst of all, you may have to eliminate jobs.

States that don't pass these harmful measures legislatively can expect to find activist-driven efforts to mandate health care coverage through the ballot initiative process. Like the 2006 wage hike initiatives, these measures often include fine print that would be confusing to voters wading through a cluttered ballot.

Damaging new health care mandates are surfacing in the states every day.

A Plan for Action

What can you do?

First, become engaged and educated. Damaging new health care mandates are surfacing in states every day. By getting involved in your state restaurant association or a well-organized and politically influential business association, you can impact the debate. Because if the health care debate goes to the ballot box, organization, discipline and a lot of fundraising is the only way to prevail.

It is next to impossible for restaurant employers to shoulder the burden of skyrocketing health premiums for their employees.

Second, educate those around you. It is imperative that as a cornerstone of the U.S. economy we educate policymakers, the media and voters. They must understand that 35 percent, on average, of the budget of a restaurant is in labor dollars. With a low profit margin that averages between 3 percent and 5 percent, it is next to impossible for restaurant employers to shoulder the burden of skyrocketing health premiums for their employees.

Third, get politically involved. With the 2008 election campaign already under way, the industry must organize and leverage its resources against anti-business forces. State and national political action committees, or PACs, support business-friendly candidates. Donating to these PACs will help ensure a viable future. And, importantly, "issues" PACs are becoming more and more critical, given the increased lawmaking-by-ballot-box trend.

The battle lines are already being drawn and sides are being taken. We need to make it clear that the restaurant industry won't roll over and play dead.

Organizations to Contact

The editors have compiled the following list of organizations concerned with the issues debated in this book. The descriptions are derived from materials provided by the organizations. All have publications or information available for interested readers. The list was compiled on the date of publications of the present volume; the information provided here may change. Be aware that many organizations may take several weeks or longer to respond to inquiries, so allow as much time as possible.

American Enterprise Institute for Public Policy Research
1150 Seventeenth St. NW, Washington, DC   20036
(202) 862-5800 • fax: (202) 862-7177
e-mail: webmaster@aei.org
Web site: www.aei.org/

The American Enterprise Institute for Public Policy Research is a privately funded organization dedicated to research and education on issues of government, politics, economics, and social welfare. Its purposes are to defend the principles and improve the institutions of American freedom and democratic capitalism, including limited government and private enterprise.

Brookings Institution
1775 Massachusetts Ave. NW, Washington, DC   20036
(202) 797-6000 • fax: (202) 797-6004
e-mail: Communications@brookings.edu
Web site: www.brookings.edu/

The Brookings Institution is a private, nonprofit organization devoted to conducting independent research, including economy research, and developing innovative policy solutions. Brookings's goal is to provide high-quality analysis and recommendations for decision makers on the full range of challenges facing an increasingly interdependent world.

The Carnegie Endowment for International Peace
1779 Massachusetts Ave. NW, Washington, DC   20036-2103
(202) 483-7600 • fax: (202) 483-1840
e-mail: info@CarnegieEndowment.org
Web site: www.carnegieendowment.org/

The Carnegie Endowment for International Peace is a private, nonprofit organization dedicated to advancing cooperation between nations and promoting active international engagement by the United States. It publishes research reports on topics such as the global economy, international labor markets and the impact of trade agreements, economic reforms in the Arab world, and the Chinese economy.

Cato Institute
1000 Massachusetts Ave. NW, Washington, DC   20001-5403
(202) 842-0200 • fax (202) 842-3490
e-mail: webmaster@cato.org
Web site: www.cato.org/index.html

The Cato Institute conducts research on public policy issues in order to promote consideration of traditional American principles of limited government, individual liberty, free markets, and peace. Topics covered in Cato Institute briefs include globalization, free trade, immigration, and Social Security.

Center for American Progress
1333 H St. NW, Washington, DC   2005
(202) 682-1611
e-mail: progress@americanprogress.org
Web site: www.americanprogress.org/

The Center for American Progress is a progressive think tank with an interest in values like diversity, shared and personal responsibility, and participatory government. It publishes broadly on economic issues, including business/regulation, credit and debt, the global economy, health care, immigration, and the environment.

Center for Strategic and International Studies
1800 K St. NW, Washington, DC   20006
(202) 887-0200 • fax (202) 775-3199
e-mail: webmaster@csis.org
Web site: www.csis.org/

The Center for Strategic and International Studies conducts research and analysis and develops policy initiatives on a broad range of issues that impact American security and the future. Its publications in the area of economics have a global focus, promoting the perspective that greater economic integration and interdependence have the potential to harmonize interests, increase wealth, and reduce conflict.

Economic Policy Institute (EPI)
1333 H St., NW, Suite 300, East Tower
Washington, DC   20005
(202) 775-8810
e-mail: researchdept@epi.org
Web site: www.epi.org

The Economic Policy Institute is a nonprofit, nonpartisan think tank that seeks to broaden the public debate about strategies to achieve a prosperous and fair economy. The economic indicators page on the EPI Web site includes current information on U.S. GDP (gross domestic product), family income, international trade and investment, jobs, and wages. Issues guides are provided on living wage, minimum wage, offshoring (job outsourcing), poverty and family budgets, retirement security, Social Security, unemployment insurance, and welfare.

Heritage Foundation
214 Massachusetts Ave. NE, Washington, DC   20002-4999
(202) 546-4400 • fax (202) 546-8328
e-mail: info@heritage.org
Web site: www.heritage.org

The Heritage Foundation is a research and educational institute that promotes conservative public policies based on the principles of free enterprise, limited government, individual freedom, traditional American values, and a strong national defense. Its Web site includes policy briefs on U.S. agriculture, the economy, health care, the federal budget and spending, labor, retirement and Social Security, as well as international trade policy and economic freedom.

Hudson Institute
1015 15th St. NW, Washington, DC   20005
(202) 974-2400
e-mail: info@hudson.org
www.hudson.org

The Hudson Institute is a nonpartisan policy research organization that aims to challenge conventional thinking and help manage strategic transitions to the future through interdisciplinary and collaborative studies in defense, international relations, economics, culture, science, technology, and law.

Institute for Policy Studies
1112 16th St NW, Suite 600, Washington, DC   20036
(202) 234-9382 • Fax (202) 387-7915
e-mail: info@ips-dc.org
www.ips-dc.org

The Institute for Policy Studies conducts research to support grassroots advocacy and the development of democratic communities. The institute's Global Economy Project focuses on the needs of workers and explores alternatives to corporate globalization of the world economy.

Institute for Public Accuracy
65 Ninth St., Suite 3, San Francisco, CA   94103
(415) 552-5378 • Fax (415) 552-6787
e-mail: institute@igc.org
Web site: www.accuracy.org/index.php

The Institute for Public Accuracy brings together diverse expertise, including policy analysts and working journalists, to broaden discussion and enhance public debate on contemporary issues, including international trade and the U.S. economy.

New America Foundation
1630 Connecticut Ave. NW, 7th Floor
Washington, DC   20009
(202) 986-2700 • fax (202) 986-3696
Web site: www.newamerica.net

The New America Foundation sponsors a wide range of research, writing, educational events, and public outreach on important global and domestic issues such as economic growth, energy and the environment, retirement, health care, trade policy, and globalization.

RAND Corporation
Office of Community Relations, RAND
Santa Monica, CA   90407-2138
(310) 393-0411, x7517
e-mail: Iao_Katagiri@rand.org
Web site: www.rand.org/

The RAND Corporation is a nonprofit research organization that performs policy analysis on critical social and economic issues such as education, poverty, crime, and the environment, as well as a range of national security issues.

U.S. Department of Labor Bureau of Labor Statistics
Postal Square Building, Washington, DC   20212-0001
(202) 691-5200
Web site: www.bls.gov/

The Bureau of Labor Statistics (BLS) is the principal fact-finding agency for the federal government in the broad field of labor economics and statistics. The BLS collects, processes, analyzes, and disseminates essential statistical data to the American public, the U.S. Congress, other federal agencies, state and local governments, business, and labor. The BLS also serves as a statistical resource to the Department of Labor.

Bibliography

Books

Daniel Altman   *Connected: 24 Hours in the Global Economy.* New York: Farrar, Straus, & Giroux, 2007.

Benjamin Barber   *Con$umed: How Markets Corrupt Children, Infantilize Adults, and Swallow Citizens Whole.* New York: W.W. Norton, 2007.

John C. Boggle   *The Battle for the Soul of Capitalism.* New Haven, CT: Yale University Press, 2005.

Sara Bongiorni   *A Year Without "Made in China": One Family's True Life Adventure in the Global Economy.* Hoboken, NJ: John Wiley & Sons, 2007.

David Callaghan   *The Cheating Culture: Why More Americans Are Doing Wrong to Get Ahead.* New York: Harcourt, 2004.

Aviva Chomsky   *"They Take Our Jobs!": And 20 Other Myths About Immigration.* Boston: Beacon, 2007.

Jonathan Cohn   *Sick: The Untold Story of America's Health Care Crisis—and the People Who Pay the Price.* New York: Harper Collins, 2007.

David Denby   *American Sucker.* New York: Little, Brown, 2005.

Thomas J.
DiLorenzo

How Capitalism Saved America: The Untold History of Our Country, From the Pilgrims to the Present. New York: Crown Forum, 2004.

Byron L. Dorgan

Take This Job and Ship It: How Corporate Greed and Brain-Dead Politics Are Selling Out America. New York: Thomas Dunne, 2006.

Peter F. Drucker

Managing in the Next Society. New York: St. Martin's, 2002.

Barbara
Ehrenreich

Bait and Switch: The (Futile) Pursuit of the American Dream. New York: Metropolitan, 2005.

Thomas L.
Friedman

The World Is Flat: A Brief History of the Twenty-First Century. New York: Farrar, Straus, & Giroux, 2005.

Olaf Gersemann

Cowboy Capitalism: European Myths, American Reality. Washington, DC: Cato Institute, 2004.

Richard Haass

The Opportunity: America's Moment to Alter History's Course. New York: Public Affairs, 2005.

Ron Hira

Outsourcing America: What's Behind Our National Crisis and How We Can Reclaim American Jobs. New York: American Management Association, 2005.

Mira Kamdar

Planet India: How the Fastest-Growing Democracy Is Transforming America and the World. New York: Scribner, 2007.

James Lardner and David A. Smith — *Inequality Matters: The Growing Economic Divide in America and Its Poisonous Consequences.* New York: New Press, 2005.

Robert H. LeBow — *Health Care Meltdown: Confronting the Myths and Fixing Our Failing System.* Chambersburg, PA: Alan C. Hood, 2004.

Alfred Lubrano — *Limbo: Blue-Collar Roots, White-Collar Dreams.* Hoboken, NJ: Wiley, 2004.

Barry C. Lynn — *End of the Line: The Rise and Coming Fall of the Global Corporation.* New York: Doubleday, 2005.

Gene Marks — *The Complete Idiot's Guide to Successful Outsourcing.* New York: Alpa, 2005.

C.K. Prahalad — *The Fortune at the Bottom of the Pyramid: Eradicating Poverty Through Profits.* Upper Saddle River, NJ: Pearson Education/Wharton School Publishing, 2005.

Jeffrey D. Sachs — *The End of Poverty: Economic Possibilities for Our Time.* New York: Penguin, 2005.

Carl J. Schramm — *The Entrepreneurial Imperative: How America's Economic Miracle Will Reshape the World (and Change Your Life).* New York: Collins, 2006.

Paul Stiles   *Is the American Dream Killing You? How "The Market" Rules Our Lives.* New York: Collins, 2005.

Periodicals

Edmund L. Andrews   "Fed Chairman Projects Soft Landing for U.S. Economy," *International Herald Tribune*, February 15, 2007.

Dennis Cauchon   "Wealth Gap Widens Between Older, Younger Americans," *USA Today*, May 21, 2007.

Daniel W. Drezner   "U.S. Trade Dilemma: Free or Fair," *Washington Post*, September 15, 2006.

Gregg Easterbrook   "Cheapskate Millionaires: The Super-Rich Have More Money than They Can Possibly Spend, So Why Do They Give So Little?" *Los Angeles Times*, March 18, 2007.

Chris Farrell   "Walling Off Growth," *Business Week*, May 31, 2006.

Charles Fishman   "The Wal-Mart Effect and a Decent Society: Who Knew Shopping Was So Important?" *Academy of Management Perspectives*, August, 2006.

Richard B. Freeman   "Does Globalization of the Scientific-Engineering Workforce Threaten U.S. Economic Leadership?" *NBER Innovation Policy and the Economy*, 2006.

Daniel Griswold   "The Fiscal Impact of Immigration
                   Reform," *Free Trade Bulletin*, May 21,
                   2007.

Laura Hartman,   "The Communication of Corporate
Robert Rubin,   Social Responsibility: United States
and K. Dhanda   and European Union Multinational
                   Corporations," *Journal of Business
                   Ethics*, October 2007.

Margaret Krome   "Farm Future Affects Urban
                   Economy, Too," *Capital Times*, May
                   16, 2007.

David Leonhardt   "U.S. Economy Is Still Growing at
and Vikas Bajaj   Rapid Pace," *New York Times*, April
                   28, 2006.

Steven Malanga   "How Unskilled Immigrants Hurt
                   Our Economy," *City Journal*, Summer
                   2006.

Bill McKibben   "Old MacDonald Had a Farmers'
                   Market—Total Self-Sufficiency Is a
                   Noble, Misguided Ideal," *In Charac-
                   ter*, Winter 2007.

Harold Meyerson   "Your Job May Not Survive," *Cincin-
                   nati Post*, May 13, 2007.

Franklin Michello "The Unemployment Effects of Pro-
and William F.   posed Changes in Social Security's
Ford   'Normal Retirement Age,'" *Business
                   Economics*, April 2006.

Paul Michael   "The Truth About a Global Market,"
Mullen   *Industrial Management*, May 2007.

Peter Navarro	"China's Influence on U.S. Economy Is Growing," *Cincinnati Post*, March 16, 2007.
Eduardo Porter	"A Soft U.S. Economy Perplexes Fed," *International Herald Tribune*, August 7, 2006.
Stephen Rose, Adam Solomon, and Anne Kim	"Talking Past the Middle," *Challenge*, January/February 2007.
Ron Scherer	"U.S. Economy Chugs Ahead Despite Auto and Housing Slumps," *Christian Science Monitor*, December 11, 2007.
Stacey L. Schreft, Aarti Singh, and Ashley Hodgson	"Jobless Recoveries and the Wait-and-See Hypothesis," *Economic Review*, 4th Quarter, 2005.
Geri Smith	"The Immigration Payoff," *Business Week*, April 19, 2006.
Shawn Tully and Corey Hajim	"Why the Private Equity Bubble Is Bursting," *Fortune*, August 20, 2007.
Christian Weller	"One Nation Under Debt," *Challenge*, January/February 2007.

Index